EDITH THE FAIR

B. W. ('Bill') Flint was born in Luton in 1935. Half-Irish, he was raised Catholic and maintained a strong faith throughout his life. Deeply passionate about literature, he started writing poetry at an early age—a collection of his poems was eventually to be published under the name William Connor Flint in 2007. While undertaking his National Service, he completed a BA in history through Leeds University, specialising in the Anglo-Saxon period; afterwards he worked as a senior marketing manager for General Motors, Vauxhall. In the 1980s Bill Flint resumed his studies, gaining a Diploma in Philosophy and Theology at Plater College, Oxford. Following this change of direction, he found fulfilment as manager of a Job-club for the disabled, while completing an MA by research through Maryvale Catholic Institute. His thesis, a theological exploration of the life and works of St Thérèse of Lisieux, was published as *The Rose of Normandie* (Lantern Tower Publications, 2007). He began his investigation into the shrine at Walsingham in 2006—work which allowed him to pursue his interests in Anglo-Saxon history, theology and literature—and he completed the work about a year before his death in September 2014. He is lovingly remembered by his wife and daughter as a devoted husband and father.

EDITH THE FAIR

VISIONARY OF WALSINGHAM

BILL FLINT

GRACEWING

First published in England in 2015
by
Gracewing
2 Southern Avenue
Leominster
Herefordshire HR6 0QF
United Kingdom
www.gracewing.co.uk

ISBN 978 085244 870 0

Typeset by Gracewing

Cover design by Bernardita Peña Hurtado

Cover image: Stained glass in the Anglican Shrine of Our Lady of Walsingham depicting the Vision of Richeldis.

Contents

Foreword

THIS PROJECT WAS undertaken after my father and I went on pilgrimage to Walsingham in the spring of 2006. I had at that time suffered a setback in my studies and was making a second attempt at university applications. My father, always whole-heartedly committed and supportive towards me, suggested that he (at the age of seventy-one) drive me from Bristol to Walsingham to ask for Our Lady's intercession. We had a long history of attending the shrine together: our first family pilgrimage had been made in 1995 when my parents and I offered petitions and we all felt the tangible, miraculous power of Our Lady's presence at the shrine. At the young age of seven, it was the first time I had experienced a direct answer to a prayer.

While driving through the beautiful countryside of Norfolk, I asked my Dad why no-one had ever tried to find out more about the identity of the Walsingham visionary, Rychold. It seemed odd that no-one had expressed an interest in carrying out an extensive work of research about a shrine that had lasted for almost one thousand years, and which was also one of the most frequented shrines of medieval Europe. 'All they would have to do was find out who the Lady of the Walsingham Manor was', I commented, 'I don't understand why someone hasn't tried to do this already.' My father informed me that the date of the shrine's foundation was in dispute and would need to be firmly established in order to identify the Lady of the Manor at the time of its foundation. Nevertheless, I had piqued his interest. We were both perplexed as to why the identity of the visionary had become obscured over time and agreed that there must be a historical reason for this. My Dad needed little encouragement to turn to one of his favourite sources: the Domesday Book. He had consulted this document at the time of my birth, naming me after the wife of the Sherriff of his home county of Bedfordshire, Azelina Tallboys.

Not long after this memorable conversation, my father and I prayed together at the Catholic Shrine and Slipper Chapel, as well as at the Holy House within the Anglican Shrine, which is also used by the Orthodox brethren of Walsingham. My father later informed me that he had promised Our Lady of Walsingham that he would investigate the identity of the Walsingham visionary if she guided me in my impending university applications. As we drove away from the shrine towards Bristol, a hare dashed across the road in front of our car. My father told me that it was certainly a sign of good luck: a comforting fact I remembered when a hare crossed my path as I walked to the cemetery in the weeks following my beloved father's death in September 2014. In the year following our memorable pilgrimage, I was accepted to study for a BA at Fitzwilliam College, Cambridge: a fact that delighted my father (the framed letter of acceptance remains on the wall of his study to this day). At this time, he committed himself to completing the work of research that he had pledged to Our Lady of Walsingham during our pilgrimage in 2006.

This book expresses many of my father's particular historical and theological interests and is an important work both for Anglo-Saxon scholars and those absorbed in the causes and after-effects of both the Norman Conquest and the English Reformation. My father re-evaluates the persistent assumption that the Norman Conquest in England was a civilising event in our nation's history, both in relation to the Anglo-Saxon Church and to the wider management of the country. He was deeply passionate about Anglo-Saxon literature and devotion, and often irritated by how the great achievements of this civilisation were overlooked in favour of the Conquest. He establishes the widespread presence of local Christian shrines across Anglo-Saxon England and ascribes their endurance to the religious practices of the local populace, as well as the greater autonomy of the individual in matters of religious devotion. He duly examines the oppression of Anglo-Saxon hagiography by Archbishop Lanfranc under William II.

In his research my father was also determined to re-establish Walsingham as an Anglo-Saxon shrine: something that the earliest Tudor commentators, Pynson and Leland, had acknowledged and which was only later disputed by historians such as J.C. Dickinson (1956). Dickinson was a scholar unspecialised in Anglo-Saxon iconography, who was also unaware of the episcopal changes that were made to the Augustinian Order of the Canons Regular, and which occurred contemporaneously with the production of the Norfolk Roll in 1130. My father claims that this Roll, in fact, refers to the establishment of Walsingham Priory and not the shrine, as Dickinson had formerly surmised. He thereby verifies the authenticity of the Pynson Ballad, which provides the earlier date of 1061. The reliability of this document had previously been brought into question as an oral narrative, but my father successfully establishes the importance of the ballad as a form of historical documentation and medieval broadcasting. One of his great passions was the significance of oral literature and he consistently claimed that the oral tradition had a longer history than the written word, and should not be overlooked by modern historians, as the authentic, contemporaneous account of the people.

In identifying the Lady of Walsingham Manor in 1061 as Edith Swanneshals, wife of Harold Godwinson (later King Harold II), my father was able to justify a fresh evaluation of Harold's claim to the throne against that of William the Conqueror. He thereby re-establishes the integrity of Harold's relationship with his predecessor, King Edward the Confessor, who supported the foundation of the shrine. His identification of Edith Swanneshals as a visionary also leads him to examine the validity of the *mores danico* marital union between Edith and Harold (previously branded as illegitimate) in the context of ancient Danish culture and the status of sacramental marriage on English shores during this period. The royal couple's good Christian character is reaffirmed through fresh research into their friendship with Saint Wulfstan of Worcester. A favourite proverb of my father's was: 'History is written by the victors'. The first time it enters my memory is on an occasion when I came home from school in a fury because my teacher had claimed that the Conqueror's invasion was justifiable on the grounds that it had widespread European support. I railed that King Edward was a canonised saint, but everyone seemed to regard his nomination of Harold Godwinson as heir as superfluous. Years on, my father surmises that the suppression of Rychold's identity as Edith Swanneshals is due to her connection with Harold II—but the shrine, as a royal foundation of King Edward the Confessor, could not be maligned by William I. The mystery we discussed years earlier in the car has been solved.

In his wider research into the history of the shrine, my father calls into question the continuing assumption that monastic corruption was widespread in England before the Reformation. He cites the pilgrimage of Erasmus, scholar of the Enlightenment and great critic of simony, as evidence of the integrity of the foundation of Walsingham. The author's research into the Augustinian Priory reveals the episcopal control of the Canons Regular and the wider communal responsibilities this entailed. The 'evidence' used against the monastic orders during the suppression of the monasteries is also brought into question. A passionate English Catholic, my father always maintained that there was a distinct difference in the conceptual values of the English and mainland European Reformations. In this context, his rereading of the iconography of Our Lady of Walsingham has great significance for the English Church. In revealing its emphasis on the Mother of God as Christ's bloodline link to the House of David, my father establishes the significance of Our Lady of Walsingham's affirmation of the temporal authority of Christ as true Man and earthly King, as well as His spiritual authority and divine kingship as true God. That in the Hebraic tradition this lineage stems from the maternal line reminds us of the significance of the maternal bloodline in Anglo-Saxon England prior to the Norman Conquest. In our final conversation my father spoke passionately of the achievements of Anglo-Saxon women. He reminded me that in a civilisation where the ruling noblemen, as trained warriors, were lucky to survive into their forties and were largely illiterate, it was highly unlikely that the great achievements of art and literature could be linked to a predominantly male community. The prejudice towards literature written by men in the English university syllabus and the common ascription of anonymous literature to men was a favourite preoccupation of mine. Few male scholars would listen with the same sympathy as my father did.

Finally, as both a patriotic Englishman and proud Catholic, my father was unwaveringly ecumenical and non-judgemental. His final assessment of Walsingham as a truly ecumenical shrine where Catholics, Anglicans and Orthodox can all trace important historical, devotional links to the visionary, Rychold, reflects his pride in the diversity of English history and the English nation. His recognition of Walsingham as an authentically royal shrine also reveals his allegiance to the English monarchy and his steadfast admiration of our current Queen, Elizabeth II. He never felt that this conflicted with his Catholic faith, or his first loyalty to the Holy Father. During his research he expressed an admiration for HRH Prince Charles's commitment to being defender 'of all religious faiths' as the proper sentiment of a truly English prince. My father, then, embraces the full complexity of English history and religious devotion, which informed his own identity. He breathes life into rich and complex aspects of our history that are commonly overlooked. I hope that after reading this book, scholars will reassess the achievements of both the Anglo-Saxon monarchy and the medieval monastic foundations prior to the Reformation, as well as the great contributions of women to our history.

This last legacy of my father is both rich and fair: not only for me, but for historians, theologians and people of faith. I can never put into words the great pride I feel in Bertram William Flint, my father: not only for his scholastic and literary achievements, but for his beautiful heart and great devotion to me as a Dad. This book reflects his lasting love for me and I only wish he were here to enjoy its lasting success.

Azelina Joan Flint, BA Hons. (Cantab.), MA (Cantab.), MA Hons. (Lond.), 2015

INTRODUCTION

THIS STUDY WAS started many years ago following a pilgrimage to the Shrine of Walsingham. The thousand-year-old historic sign, a shrine of living faith celebrating the Annunciation to Our Blessed Lady, was glorious in late spring sunshine and the peace of rural Norfolk, a place of living history. Yet the Founder Visionary of Walsingham was still unknown and unidentified in the historic narrative.

The Lady of the Manor named in the Pynson Ballad is known as 'Rychold', a legendary figure without any substance in history apart from this single attribution in the Pynson Ballad. Her identity is a mystery, which is indeed intriguing, as the person who received such an ecstatic and sublime vision is described as the 'Lady of the Manor' and is therefore a person of some local substance who would have been well known to her contemporaries. However, she is and has been for many centuries an unnamed person without any historic identity. The Ballad identifies her as 'Rychold', Lady of Walsingham Manor of Walsingham, but provides no further evidence of her historic identity.

From the reign of Henry III from 1 October 1207 to 16 November 1272, until the time of Henry VIII, royal patronage became a principal factor in the international fame of this Shrine of Our Lady of the Annunciation. The religious, political and economic importance of this Shrine is an intriguing factor in the visionary founder's historic identity, which, on the face of it, appears to have been unrecorded.

However, the Domesday Book clearly records that in 1061 the Manor of Walsingham was the residence of King Harold, who held it as part of his wife's family estates and therefore at the time of the shrine's foundation, Edith (his wife) was most probably 'The Lady of the Manor'. As Harold's widow in 1066, it is clear that this holding had been part of the Norfolk holdings of Edith's mother Wulfgyth (or Wulfhilda), daughter of Aethelred the Unready, who was the widow of Ulfketel Snoring (sometimes spelt 'Ulfcytel Snillingri'). After his death at the Battle of Assundan, where Thorkell Havi won a famous victory with the army of King Canute, she probably became the wife of Thorkell the Tall under the laws of chivalry. Edith was, therefore, as widow of King Harold, a threat to the Norman dynasty through her sons, and in 1070 fled to the protection of her father or stepfather in Denmark, Thorkell the Tall. There is no clear evidence as to the paternity of Edith, although she is clearly the daughter of Wulfgyth (her maternal line is undisputed) and either Ulfketel or Thorkell the Tall.

In 1487, King Henry VII made a three-day pilgrimage to the Shrine of Our Lady of the Annunciation, prior to his last famous battle (the battle of Stoke Field, 16th June 1487). This was the second year of his reign and he died in 1509. This final victory over the remaining Lancastrian forces resulted in the establishment of the Tudor dynasty. This most favourable outcome was celebrated by the King by installing his battle standard in the Walsingham Shrine chapel, a gift of great distinction. The Walsingham Shrine became most honoured from this time of the consolidation of the

Tudor dynasty as an important royal shrine, founded in the time of Edward the Confessor.

It had been from the beginning a royal shrine and had been much honoured by every English monarch from at least Henry III. Henry VII, who commissioned the printing of the Ballad, added that any that were 'learned' in this matter should come forward and record it with the Chronicler, and therefore it was partly upon this royal command that I began my own research. The Walsingham Shrine is of European and international importance. It is the first shrine dedicated to 'The Annunciation' with a history of English royal patronage and yet unknown (except by its attribution in the Pynson Ballad) as having been founded during the reign of Edward the Confessor in 1061. My research was unfruitful until I decided to scrutinise the Little Domesday of Norfolk (which was compiled in 1088) and discovered that the manor of Great Walsingham was land owned by Harold Godwin, King of England, and in 1066, following his defeat at the Battle of Hastings, it is recorded as 'Land of the King', William I, in the Norfolk Domesday Book.

Harold was married to Edith Swanneshals and her name and patronage warranted the title Rychold: her mother Wulfgyth was daughter of Aethelred the Unready and was half-sister or sister to King Edward; Edith's mother had owned all the Walsingham holdings and her sons (Ketel and Ulfketel) owned Little Walsingham and Great Snoring at the time of the Norman Conquest. Thus, it is probable that the Visionary of Walsingham was indeed Queen Edith, daughter of Wulfgyth and Thorkell the Tall, as set out below, with supporting evidence taken from the will of Wulfgyth and records of the Domesday Book. The

Pynson Ballad, the Victoria County History (hereafter VCH) for Norfolk and a variety of other sources (such as the Elmenham list of Bishops, which record Aelfwine as Bishop) furnish cross-references to Wulfgyth's will, and there exists a great quantity of supporting detail from a variety of sources. This investigation was renewed following a visit to the Shrine of Our Lady of Walsingham with my daughter in the summer of 2006. During this visit, I committed myself, on the successful outcome of my daughter's scholastic ambitions, to write a book that would hopefully reveal to the reader and myself the name of the 'Lady of Walsingham Manor' who is recorded as 'Rychold' in the Pynson Ballad.

It was widely accepted that the Shrine was built upon the detailed instructions given by Our Lady to 'Rychold' in the year 1061, as recorded in the ballad printed at the command of Henry VII *c.* 1494 or earlier. This date of the founding of the Shrine was verified by John Leland, antiquary to King Henry VIII.

I chose to challenge the dating and misunderstandings of J.C. Dickinson.[1] The book sold 164 copies, and in my judgement is highly contentious regarding the postulation of a late date of the foundation of the Shrine to *c.* 1130 or thereabouts. However, this decision to challenge the suppositions in this work was, upon preliminary review by some commentators, opposed on the grounds of insufficient evidence; therefore, in the introduction I have shown this late dating to be founded on poor evidence, ignorance of the iconography, and clear misunderstanding of the timing and fiscal arrangements required by crusaders undertaking the Cross, especially that part of the Crusades marshalled in England, Scotland and Wales during the time of the late Norman and early Angevin dynasties.

Only when I had completed this task of critical review was I then at liberty to embark upon this attempt to reveal the identity of Rychold, 'Lady of Walsingham Manor' in 1061, who received the Walsingham Visions in early spring, probably May, the Marian month of that august year. This date coincides with the English campaigns in the Marches and north Wales led by Earl Harold, where, acting directly for King Edward, he subdued the Welsh.

One of very few sound written evidences from this time is the Little Domesday book (hereafter LDB), upon whose testament we can rely. This book not only provides the names of the owner of this manor in 1066: it also provides the names of the title-holder before the time of the Norman Conquest, and therefore often reveals the name of the owner in 1061.

To the diligent researcher, on careful analysis it is irrefutable that the Lady of the Manor at this time was the wife of Earl Harold, who, in 1066, was proclaimed King of England. His wife, Edith 'Swanneshals', also known as Edith the Fair and Rich, is thus referred to in the Ballad as 'Rychold': that is, 'fair and rich'. It follows that it would be necessary to carry through a detailed review as far as possible into the origin and meaning of the Pynson Ballad in all its detail, and carefully analyse the etymology and linguistic and oral sources of the printed version, but also to endeavour to reveal, in its earlier written vernacular and oral versions, both its character and story. I leave it to others to pass judgement on my efforts.

It then followed that from this evidential beginning that I could precede to a more general historical research procedure into the lives of Harold and Edith. Their married life, under the prevailing system of *mores danico,* has been quite wrongly maligned, implying an illicit union unsanctified by the English Church.

I demonstrate this to be in error of the facts as understood by the ruling classes of this period. For instance, it is now widely accepted that Harold was not married to a person known in her day as Edith of Clywed, wife of Gryffydd Llewellyn, and that he did not sire two male children with her.[2] Edith was married to a Welsh prince and did not have any claim to a royal title. This illustrates the degree to which later commentators were mistaken and misled in dishonouring Harold and his hand-fast spouse, Edith the Fair and Rich.

Edith Swanneshals, on the other hand, is known from Danish sources to have been the daughter of Thorkell the Tall and Wulfgyth, daughter of the English King Aethelred the Unready and therefore a niece of King Edward. She is referred to as a fabulously wealthy and beautiful young woman and was a court favourite of both King Canute, through her father Thorkell the Tall, and King Edward, who was married to Harold's sister and related to her through her mother, the daughter of King Aethelred (who was therefore a sister or half-sister to King Edward). Through her daughter, Gytha (who, according to Scandinavian sources married Monomakh 'The Rus', Founder of modern Russia), she is therefore directly related to our present Queen Elizabeth II of the House of Windsor, together through a more distant lineage with the Duke of Edinburgh, which links both spouses of the current House of Windsor to Edith the Fair and Harold, and, through their ancient lineage, to Alfred the Great.

It has not been possible to follow a chronological pattern in carrying through this project, and therefore I have used the most ancient pattern of historical storytelling by using a linked episodic carousel approach related to the central hub of the Shrine's foundational date of 1061, together with personal episodic glimpses of the lives of Harold and Edith 'Rychold Swanneshals', who is indicated by examination of contemporary accounts to be the founder of the royal shrine. The Saxon blood line of Aethelred and his son Edward the Confessor includes their half-sister Wulfgyth, who, as Edith's mother was of the Saxon bloodline, whose lands (prior to 1066 and 1068 when the Norfolk LDB was published) included the Manor of Walsingham, adjacent to the holdings of Edward and his close kinsmen.

The identity of the visionary who was the Lady of the Manor of Walsingham, who prayed to Mary the mother of God as recorded in the Pynson Ballad, is known in current literature by the name of Rychold or its variants. It is recorded in the Pynson Ballad that she was given some task to perform in Our Lady's honour, and is referred to here as 'Rychold', and for at least eight centuries has been known by this name. All the literature from both Anglican and Catholic sources throughout the world has referred to her by this name or one of its many variations. However, research into the derivation and its etymological and linguistic sources has been largely unsuccessful. Other than a personal feminine name meaning 'Rich' or well-favoured (such as used by Edith Swanneshals, wife of Harold, also known as Edith 'rich and fair'), as a family name this is not well documented.[3] However, the founding date of the Shrine has been challenged by

Dickinson and others, and we need to firmly establish a date of foundation in order to conduct our enquiry into the person named Rychold in the Pynson Ballad.

The Norfolk Roll of 1130–1 has a reference to Rychold Faverques, as cited by J.C. Dickinson, and assumes a date for the founding of both the Shrine and Priory as very close or contiguous, dating the foundation of the Shrine to *c.* 1130.[4] However, the Priory erected by the Austin Friars was a foundation largely determined by the episcopal changes that occurred following the long dispute with Archbishop Stigand, whose Norfolk residence was, until 1071 the ancient Saxon Cathedral of Elmenham. This ancient Norfolk bishopric was first transferred to Thetford under dispute; it had been held by Stigand's brother Aelfwine from 1032–1047 and then by Stigand himself subsequently on two separate occasions but with the support of the High Sheriff Roger Bigot, who also tried unsuccessfully later to have the see moved to Bury St Edmunds. It was transferred to Norwich before any building took place at Thetford in 1094. The Augustinian Order of the Canons Regular was and remains canons in congregation under the jurisdiction of the local bishop. The transfer of crown lands to episcopal jurisdiction required the consent of the King's representative in the transfer of guardianship and land occupancy of this royal Shrine. The Manor of Walsingham is clearly the King's land as recorded in the LDB dated 1088. Therefore the assumptions made as to the Shrine's foundational dates are misplaced, as any such foundation after the Conquest would have had to have received the royal seal and ecclesiastical approval. It is also of note that the Pynson Ballad, as set out below, relates a precise date year for the foundation as 1061.

That is prior to the Conquest, and as a private foundation of 'The Lady of the Manor' according to Pynson, both the chapel dedicated to Laurence and the Shrine chapel could not have been built after the Conquest. Pynson's royal employer who commissioned the printing from existent written sources was King Henry VII, following his victory in the decisive battle of Stoke. After his victory, he sent the Royal Banner to Walsingham in tribute to Our Lady of Walsingham, where it remained until the vandalism of the dissolution. It is only as a private foundation dating from the time of Edward the Confessor that the Shrine could have been founded: otherwise, it would not have had royal status.

After 1066, the shrine would have been a royal foundation of Norman patronage; the understanding that this shrine was founded under the Angevin dynasty is unsupported and extremely unlikely, taking into account the Norman suppression of these English places of holiness. Moreover, the date that Dickinson conjectures of 1130 during the reign of Stephen contradicts both the Pynson Ballad and John Leland. Further, the turmoil and uncertainty surrounding Mathilda's claim to the throne and subsequent hostilities are an unlikely setting for the Shrine's foundation. Dickinson also infers that a Lady who was called Rychold Faverches owned the manor and entailed it to her underage son, Geoffrey. This cannot be the case as the Manor was a royal holding requiring the signatures of the High Sheriffs for this action to be transacted without royal approval, and as this was (and is still) a royal landholding, this is most unlikely. In the Book of Hours, University Library Cambridge, it is recorded that the original chapel was founded in 1061.[5] I quote from Dickinson: 'The very fine cartulary of Walsingham Priory now in the British Museum furnishes a list of Priors giving both their names and their periods in office. Which establishes that the building of the Priory in Walsingham began in or about the year 1153 and this is attested by other evidence'.[6]

The Pynson Ballad records that the Priory of Walsingham was preceded by a chapel built in honour of Our Lady by 'Rychold'. A person described as Geoffrey was the tenant landholder who may have assisted in converting the original Chapel into the Augustinian Priory. This is confirmed by Geoffrey's Foundation Charter and may be taken as authentic.

Dickinson's statement is an error, in that the Pynson Ballad (as shown below in chapter 3) uses the name Rychold, and nowhere refers to Faverques. The ballad does not refer to the priory in any way whatsoever; nor does the Pynson Ballad in any other matter refer to Rychold's son. Further to these errors, the Charter referred to as the Geoffrey's Foundation Charter is in fact the instrument at Law through which Geoffrey's clerk at the Shrine is empowered to carry out arrangements for funding any eventuality and the passing of Land Title to the jurisdiction of the Bishop of Norwich, and subsequently into the administration of the Augustinian Friars.[7]

It is clear and unequivocal that this Charter was in practice a way of raising funds by those 'taking the Cross' and was drafted as the instrument for Geoffrey, who was the Walsingham tenant of the Crown at that time regarding the foundation of the Priory, and not the original Shrine, which must have already been in existence in order to support Edwy, who was clearly a priest in charge of the Shrine and probably an Augustinian Clerk (as he is referred to in this Charter document). This Charter does not refer to the Shrine's foundation with its dedicated Chapel and iconic statue of Our Lady of the Annunciation.

Dickinson continues, 'of Richelde little is known but we have in the Pipe Roll 1130–31 an invaluable note which suggests that she was a widow in this year. This tells us that one William de Houghton rendered account for ten gold Marks for the right to have Richelde Fervaques as his wife, with her land, and to have the wardship of her son until the latter became a knight and afterwards the son was to hold the land from William.'[8] This is a classic way of raising funds by mortgage of land and property which remains entailed to the son on achieving knighthood as a Crusader. Thus we can understand clearly how the widow of Geoffrey of Faverques became the fund-holder of her son, and his guardianship responsibilities over the Shrine of Walsingham.

Dickinson goes on: 'It is difficult to avoid the conclusion that the Geoffrey here mentioned is the father of the founder of Walsingham Priory and the widow mentioned 'Richelde' who built the Chapel there.' This partial understanding of the Charter, including misinterpretation of dates and crusader situations, is shown to be entirely without foundation. Dickinson continues: 'One Geoffrey is mentioned in 1108 along with William de Houghton and who also witnesses the Charter of Binham Priory (1101–1112). A little later Binham recovered a moiety of Walsingham against Geoffrey and his Priest Warin and Geoffrey witnessed a gift to Castle Acre before 1130, but the Pipe Roll shows that he was dead by 1131. So quite clearly it was a namesake of his that founded the Priory of Walsingham confirmed to the Bishop of Norwich in 1153.'[9] Clearly, this is unsatisfactory, as there is no evidence whatsoever for a 'namesake'. The Geoffrey Charter, providing that it is properly understood, was an instrument empowering Edwy (his clerk) to carry through the passing on of the guardianship of the Shrine at such time as jurisdiction was confirmed to the Bishop of Norwich, which is recorded as occurring in 1153. Dickinson then pontificates: 'This is significant indeed because to have witnessed a Charter the person would have to be born before 1130.' We read: 'This entry implies that Geoffrey II could not have been born before 1100 at the very earliest; a fact which tells very strongly against a foundation date of the Chapel at Walsingham of 1061 (as a child could not found a Chapel).' There is an unsupported assumption here by the author that the Rychold of the Ballad is the same person as Richelde named on the Pipe Roll of 1130–1131. The writer goes on to say that there is no authority for a date earlier than the fifteenth century; this is an erroneous assumption when we examine the evidences. The Pynson Ballad, as shown in chapter 3, from its preprint existence, is derived from an oral and chronicler tradition as of the second half of the eleventh century.

Further, Henry VIII's antiquarian and archivist, John Leland, whose work is widely acknowledged as an accurate record of evidences available to him in the sixteenth century, in his work *Collectanea,* records that the original chapel was built in 1061 in the time of Edward the Confessor.[10] Leland's work has rarely been questioned or found to be inaccurate. Therefore, both Leland and the ballad contradict such a bold statement.[11]

It must be stressed that women did not habitually take their husbands' surnames in the middle ages; this is a relatively modern practice dating from late Tudor times. Primogeniture was not a matter of common or ecclesiastical law. Women could inherit great wealth and land: for instance, Edith Swanneshals, who inherited through her father Thorkell Havi, and Queen Edith, who inherited from her father Ralph Earl of Wessex. The name appended was usually the familial relationship 'daughter-of'; this was common in the area of the Danelaw and prevalent throughout Scandinavia.

The name Rychold or Richeldis has a variety of meanings, ranging from 'fair', 'gracious' and 'beautiful' to plain 'rich'. Faverches is probably the name of a place in Normandy adjacent to Lisieux and indicates the place of family residence or land ownership from which a source of wealth flowed. It cannot be used as a surname indicating an earlier marriage as is the modern custom, but would denote, for instance, a land-holding from which personal wealth accrued. It may indicate a place of family residence or wealth relating to a father or a husband. It is also important to raise the matter of Richeldis Faverches. I quote from Dickinson's descriptive use as 'miles fundatur'; the Medieval Latin word *fundatur* in the context of these deeds should be understood as the major fund-holder or provider of funds through the provision of rents and not the founder of a place or building such as the Walsingham chapel. The word derives from the meaning 'source of a river as in the headwaters of a tributary'.

In order to assist the reader in this understanding, I quote from the Bull issued in 1145 by Pope Eugenius III: it was issued from Vetralla on 1 December 1145 and called for the second Crusade. It addresses his illustrious son, Louis King of the Franks, and all his faithful sons living in Gaul. Those who took the vow were to be granted the following indulgence:

> For the remission of penance, the protection of wives and children and possessions and freedom from legal action from the time of the taking of the Cross, until their return or death, cancellation to pay interest on debts and permission to mortgage property in order to have funds for the journey.

Louis II soon became the focus of the Second Crusade. His queen, Eleanor of Aquitaine, and the Bishops of Noyon, Langres and Lisieux were prominent supporters, indicating Lisieux as a place of importance to the Crusade, together with Thierry of Alsace, the Count of Flanders, who headed the List of Crusaders. Among many dozens of counts and nobles, William of Warrenne, Earl of Surrey and landholder in Norfolk, took the Cross and led the English contingent that left Dartmouth on 14 May 1147.

From this Papal Bull is derived the legal instrument used by crusaders to safeguard their households in their absence and explains how Geoffrey's deed was made in response to this papal edict. It does not imply that he was intent on passing ownership at this time to the Austin Canons, but was leaving the matter in the hands of his priest in charge of the Shrine in Walsingham. In no manner does it suggest that he or a relative founded the Shrine. It also implies that Geoffrey was strongly connected to the Norman French party with mortgaged lands in the area of Lisieux.

The Lady of Walsingham carried out our Lady's command, having been the recipient in prayer of a detailed vision, and is known therefore as 'The Visionary'. I point out that the visionaries of the Shrine of Knock in Ireland are largely unknown and, for example, Saint Bernadette Soubirous of Lourdes left the area of her birth because she was only carrying through Our Lady's wishes and had no desire to become the object of attention in the matter of the Shrine's foundation; she was, as she said 'carrying out Our Lady's commands'. There can be little doubt that this was also the case for the Visionary of Walsingham. The great message of the Annunciation is that Jesus was true man born of Mary by the Holy Spirit. The Shrine was erected by the Lady of The Manor and a Chapel built to provide shelter for the replica and statue of Our Lady and the Infant Crowned Jesus at some later date as protection against the weather.

This would have been carried through probably prior to the winter of 1061 or 1062. The existing Chapel for the manor dedicated to Saint Laurence was still in place at the time of Our Lady's foundation and is shown in the Lee Warner drawing in Dickinson's book. Chapels dedicated to Saint Laurence are invariably, as indicated by plate 3b, Anglo Saxon, of late English construction which preceded the Norman and supports an early date of 1061 as in Dickinson's work.[12]

Laurence was a Roman martyr, Deacon of the Roman Church; he was martyred by Valerian in 258. Constantine the Great, raised to Holy Roman Emperor in these islands, was the first to erect a small oratory over his burial place, 'outside the walls' of Rome. Laurence was therefore an honoured saint for the Anglo-Saxon Church and nobility, who were much inspired by the English connections of Constantine. The private Chapel dedicated to him is pictured in Dickinson's book and the photograph clearly shows the doorway to be in the very late English style with a hint of early round-arched Norman construction. It is recorded by the 'Commissioners' of the dissolution that the Chapel to Saint Laurence, which was incorporated into the north-east wall of the Priory nave, and was still venerated as part of the Shrine where small donations were listed as donated by pilgrims, thus confirming the Anglo-Saxon origins of the Shrine. This links the foundation to Harold and his wife Edith the fair and rich, in support of the early date of 1061.

A note to the Rolls of 1130 says that the son of a lady called Richeldis (that is, very rich) on coming of age will have the name of the original founder of the chapel (i.e. Richeldis), which is the same name as Edith Swanneshals, Lady of Walsingham Manor in 1066 and before. It is clear that Geoffrey's mother was not the Shrine's founder but a major provider of funds necessary to maintain the buildings and pilgrims and fund the Augustinian priest who served the Shrine and parish, because the dates ascribed to her are incompatible with the date of this chapel and the records of Walsingham in the LDB. Further to this, it is through her funding that the Priory will be endowed. The chapel of Saint Laurence is clearly late English, dating to the first half of the eleventh century, supported by a plate in Dickinson.[13]

Further to this, John Leland is reliable in recording that some Austin Canons were introduced following the Coronation of William. Although Canons Regular was established in the fifth century, they were subject to many changes throughout Europe and the renewed Congregations in Hereford, Lynn, Bristol and elsewhere were Canons Regular. We note that William of Coventry, in his Chronicle AD 620, records, 'Paulinus with twelve clerics were sent by the Pope to assist Augustine'.[14] Dr Lingard states: 'In many of these Cathedral and Minster establishments the Clergy had been Canons Regular from the beginning. In some they had been monks but had reordered themselves to Canons regular.'[15] In his history of archbishops, Diceto writes that, at St Dunstan's suggestion, King Edgar expelled clerics from most establishments and replaced them with monks. Speaking of Aefric, a monk who had been elected Archbishop of Canterbury, the Anglo-Saxon Chronicle AD 995 records that when he came to his Cathedral he was received by a company of Clerics when he would have preferred monks.[16]

In the eleventh century, there was a revival in northern Europe of the Canons Regular (for example, the Vincentians in France), and it was these renewed congregations which followed the Conqueror and established new houses in Britain. It was doubtless the revival of this ancient order to which Leland refers.[17]

In the VCH record of the Priors of Pontney, Bishop William de Turbe (of Norwich Diocese) is shown as Bishop from 1145–1174. Geoffrey occurs in 1167 in History of Archbishop Becket Rolls Series VI. 262; these references are all a hundred years or so after the founding of the Shrine.[18]

The earliest deeds in the Cartularies of Walsingham Priory refer to Richeldis, the mother of Geoffrey de Faverches, as founder of the chapel. The note in the VCH of Norfolk comments that the term 'founding' in the deeds refers to the re-establishment or rebuilding of the chapel after the Conquest. This surely refers to the reordering of a private chapel and not the foundation of the Shrine.

The date 1169 is given as the day on which Geoffrey Faverches set out on pilgrimage to Jerusalem. This is probably a mistake, as the Second Crusade left England under command of William de Warrenne in

1147.[19] This note in the VCH of Norfolk is described as a calculation arrived at from careful study of the years recorded of different priors' rule, as given from the dateless Charter Lists.

However, 'The second Crusade set out on 27th April 1147 for Dartmouth. When the men of Flanders, Frisia, Normandy and Cologne set out for England and joined the Scottish, Welsh and English Crusaders. They left Dartmouth on May 19th 1147.'[20] It is therefore apparent that the careful study of dates in this regard is in need of revision. The first Crusade was too early for the person Geoffrey referred to if he was of the age accredited to him by Dickinson, and the third crusade far too late. This Charter list in terms of dating thus appears to be impossible with any degree of accuracy.

The dates of the major crusades in this period were: the First Crusade, 1096–1099; the second 1144–1155; and the third, 1187–1192. Further, it is clear that the Chapel of Our Lady of Walsingham in 1130–1150 was of no small repute before the priory was built. It is rare in Norfolk for a Manorial private chapel to have possession of tithes and land benefactions. Therefore, we can safely assume the Shrine to be of considerable age covering at least three generations for this kind of endowment to have accumulated in these times. This reasonable assumption again supports the earlier date of 1061. The Cartulary in the British Museum also has a list of priors, indicating that the Priory Chapel replacing the original was started around 1153.

The Charter is recorded in the time of William Turbe, Bishop of Norwich 1146–1175. Dickinson writes: 'It is curious that, whereas Geoffrey Faverches' foundation Charter referring to the new Priory Chapel the regular life being initiated by 'my Clerk Edwy' the confirmation by Roger Bigot (at possibly a later date) records, my clerks of Walsingham Ralph and Geoffrey, instituting the new order there.'[21] This is presumably a reference to lay clerks of the Canons Regular and is possibly a reference to Harold's tenure at the Manor before 1066: he and his wife Edith were strongly associated with the Order from their endowment of Waltham Priory, which was given to Harold by King Canute in, probably, 1022. It points to the fact that the Canons were already administering the Shrine as a private foundation prior to the transfer of the property to the bishopric of Norwich sometime after 1147: probably 1053. Dickinson writes: 'According to a late note in the Cartulary Geoffrey de Faverches 'forwyth the chyrche' of the said Priory and he gave it to the Chapel of Our Lady with all the ground within the site of the said church.'[22]

There follows the bequest that affirms that the Shrine was outside the jurisdiction of the ecclesiastical authorities of the Norman and Angevin dynasties, which indicates an early date of the visions prior to the Conquest as the probable foundation date. Otherwise, the Norman ecclesiastical authorities would certainly have used such a holy foundation as signifying approval for the Conquest, which had been conducted under the tacit approval of the papal banner, or alternatively suppressed the shrine as of Anglo-Saxon origin and made it a matter of local jurisdiction, for which there is no evidence.

The seal and badges of the Shrine of Our Lady of Walsingham are also unlikely to date from the late Norman-Angevin period. The pictorial representations of the *Jesse Tree* show a symbolic tree or vine with spreading branches that represent the genealogy in line with Isaiah's prophecy.

This understanding was expressed by the twelfth-century monk Hervaeus thus: 'The patriarch Jesse belonged to the royal family of Judah. That is why the root of Jesse signifies the lineage of Kings. The Rod signifies Mary and the flower Jesus.'[23] The first representations of the passage taken from Isaiah, 11:1, read: 'There shall come forth a shoot from the stump of Jesse and a branch shall grow out from his roots.' The following is taken from the Vulgate Bible, used in the Middle Ages: 'Et egredietur virga de radice Jesse et flos de radice eius ascendet'. This can be translated as: 'and there shall come forth a Rod from the stem of Jesse and a branch shall grow up from his root.'

The earliest representations date from the beginning of the eleventh century and show the shoot in the form of a straight stem or a flowering branch held in the hand, most often of the Virgin Mary with Jesus held by Mary, sometimes pointing to the flowering branch: this is exactly as shown on the Walsingham icon. See Sermon 24 of Saint Leo the Great: 'In which rod, no doubt the Blessed Virgin Mary is predicted, who sprung from the stock of Jesse and David and fecundated by the Holy Spirit brought forth a new flower of human flesh becoming a Virgin Mother'.[24]

The first representations of this passage of Isaiah date from about AD 1000 in the West, showing a shoot in the form of a straight stem on a flowering branch held in the hand (most often) of the Virgin. Jesus is sometimes held by Mary or Isaiah or other ancestral figures. The shoot as an attribute acted as a reminder of the prophecy (the New hidden in the Old, the Old revealed in the New). In the Byzantine world, these figures appear as a normal-looking tree; in the background of the Nativity scenes, they act as a reminder to the viewer of the prophecy of Isaiah. This iconic representation therefore supports the early date of 1061 following the Roman tradition. We have the famous window in Chartres Cathedral dated precisely to 1145, which, had the Shrine been founded in 1130, would probably have used this iconic depiction of Isaiah's prophetic fulfilment. In fact, in northern Europe the Tree with extended branches is most common; whereas in the Holy Lands, especially the western patriarchies, they show the Crowned Virgin as the most prominent teaching. The seals as depicted in Dickinson's book show this early image, with the Christ Jesus pointing to the Flowering Jesse Tree, held by Mary, who is crowned. This statue and the seals are of immense importance, confirming that Christ is not only the Eternal King: he is also Universal King and as head of the Church reigns over all. Christians are therefore 'a kingly people' and anointed Christian monarchs are subject to his earthly rule just as they are to his eternal sovereignty. This is not an understanding that kings wanted to acknowledge, because it would project great power to the Church and the lords Spiritual; the Norman Conqueror and most monarchs who succeeded him sought to establish the earthly Crown's supremacy, confirming their right to appoint Bishops.

The early Walsingham seals in the British Museum and the University of Oxford provide us with a very important iconographic representation of Our Lady with her son Jesus. She is enthroned and wearing the Davidic Crown; Jesus is sitting on her left knee holding a Bible open at the prophecy of Isaiah and points with his right hand to the Tree of Jesse. Mary's throne with the seven sacramental scrolls on the upright chair-back supports illustrates the Sacramental Church with Jesus as True Man and True God, 'The Word Made Flesh'. Thus Mary residing on the seat of wisdom is also Mother of His Church. The Tree of Jesse represents in this art-form the genealogy of Jesus as the descendant of David through Mary as conceived by the Holy Spirit. The Patriarch Jesse was of the Royal House; therefore, as the father of King David, it depicts the fulfilment of the prophecy of the coming of the Davidic Messiah. This understanding of the Messianic fulfilment is a teaching of the very early fathers, including Tertullian, who uses this understanding to confirm the belief that Jesus was True God and True Man.

The understanding that Jesus is the Davidic Messiah is a most important revelation of His authority on earth. Christ the King is a descendant through His Mother of the House of David, and this was an important factor in medieval understanding. Thus the reformists who placed secular rulers over the Catholic Church of Jesus Christ did so by denying the exulted place of Mary His Virgin Mother. This is compelling evidence that supports an early date of the founding of the Shrine of Our Lady of Walsingham. This iconic representation is of the early eleventh century type, which has its understanding and historic provenance from the early Fathers and was prevalent in the Western Patriarchy and Italy and therefore it strongly supports the date of founding as 1061, or at the very least in the reign of Edward the Confessor revealed to Edith Rich and Fair who was probably related through her mother (Wulfgyth) to Edward, thus enjoying some real form of protection by William in 1066 despite being the wife and Queen of King Harold. The very elaborate genealogical tree depictions shown in the

Jesse Tree window of Chartres Cathedral date to 1145, and give credence to the spiritual message incorporated in the Incarnation and the disputes regarding church and state relationships at this time.

The theological message and teaching of the Walsingham Shrine is not fully appreciated unless we hold and understand Our Lady's message that she is the ancestral matriarch of the Davidic Messiah. As Jesus was a Jew, it is also a timely reminder that to be of true lineage it is the matriarchal line which is essential according to the Jews. Moreover, it explains why, at the height of the Reformation in England, this most venerated statue was taken to London and publicly burnt. It was probably at the command of the Royal Household of Henry VIII that this was carried through, despite four hundred years of veneration, to the great sadness and sorrow of many. This teaching of the Fathers and understanding of the medieval Church of England was ridiculed by many reformists; the underlying theology of Jesus the Davidic Messiah, the Universal King, was contrary to their claim of secular royal authority having sovereignty over the Church Catholic.

Dickinson reports that the Statue of Our Lady resembles Our Lady of Rocamadour; this ancient statue of the Shrine of Rocamadour shows our Lady wearing the Davidic Crown and is dated to the ninth and tenth centuries. This is despite the fact that it cannot be dated with any precision because it has been subject to fire damage, which indicates that the Scriptural revelation of Mary as descendant of Jesse has great antiquity in the Christian Church. Therefore, it supports the early foundation of the Walsingham Shrine, in that it is the earliest form of Our Lady crowned, holding the flowering stump of the Tree of

Jesse. The Statue of Our Lady currently on display at the Shrine of Rocamadour is a twelfth-century copy of the original ninth- or tenth-century icon. The form of iconography at Walsingham dates from the very early eleventh century. The overriding evidence therefore supports the understanding confirmed by Leland and Pynson that the Shrine was founded by Our Lady of The Annunciation in 1061 in the reign of Edward.[25]

Dickinson makes a fundamental error in describing the so-called Geoffrey Foundation Charter in reference to the founding of the Walsingham Shrine, as opposed to (or in conjunction with) the exclusive Foundation Charter signed by Roger Bigot and de Clare in 1153. In the VCH it is recorded of the Abbey of St Benet of Holme that 'it was awarded King Cnut's patronage from 1019. The Saxon Nobles Ralph the Staller and Edric the King's Steersman were benefactors together with Edith Swanneshals' of the Abbey.[26] Edward continued this royal patronage and supported the Abbey with large donations from 1046. Edward's land-holdings are clearly shown in the LDB and also in the map titled Norfolk Western Hundreds in the Domesday Book.[27] This supports the understanding that Edith Swanneshals, wife of Harold, was an important member of the court of King Cnut as guardian or daughter of Thorkell Havi, and also at the court of King Edward. She is listed as an important benefactor of the Abbey, although the benefactor's list is not dated. The lists of benefactors were recorded and sometimes recited in the prayers of the congregation as part of the prayers of the choir monks on specified remembrance days dedicated to the memory of benefactors. Finally, I quote from Dickinson: 'The Pynson Ballad records a chapel built to house the 'The House of The Annunciation' following the Shrine's foundation' and sometime before the Austin Priory was built probably in 1153.[28] The Pynson Ballad, therefore, is not 'late evidence', but, although published in the 1490s, was written, as I demonstrate below, over a lengthy period in the Norman and early Angevin times 1066–1130.

The Walsingham Cartulary (Cartulary fo. 8r =Mon.) I have transcribed as follows:

> *Notum sit vobis me dedisse et concessisse Deo S. Mariae et Edwino clerico meo, et ordinum religionis, quem ipse providerit instituendum, capellam quam mater mea fundauit in Walsingham in honore perpetuae Virginis Mariae, una cum possessione ecclesiae Omnium Sanctorum ejusdem villae.*

This Chapel which houses the miraculous house is, therefore, administered and funded by Geoffrey's mother, which funding includes the upkeep of Edwino the Cleric in ordinary, who is most probably an Augustinian and who is the Shrine's director, and also provides the services of parish priest, all of which is well understood until such times as the Shrine Chapel passes to the Diocesan authority in this case of Bishop Turbe in 1053. I would point out that both Harold as landholder in 1061 and his wife Edith Swanneshals who were given Waltham Abbey by Cnut, endowed and rebuilt it under Edward the Confessor; they were devoted to Saint Laurence, as adjacent to the later Abbey they had a Chapel built in his honour.

Hugh Bigod, the feudatory and Royal Steward, testified that, in his presence together with three other knights, Henry I on his death bed disinherited his daughter, Maud, and designated Stephen his successor. Stephen was crowned on 22 December 1135. Thus, Hugh Bigod or his successor as signature to the Confirmation Charter of 1153 was a fervent supporter of Stephen and the understanding that it was during his turbulent reign that the Shrine was founded is not credible.

In the VCH of Norfolk, there is a note that the Pynson Ballad in the Pepys Library is a unique copy and is dated 1460; this appears to refer to a printed version and again states that the Shrine of Our Lady of Walsingham was founded in 1061 in the reign of Edward the Confessor.[29] The earliest deeds in the Cartulary of Walsingham Priory name Richeldis (the mother of Geoffrey de Favraches) as the founder of the Chapel. The word 'founder' refers to the reestablishment of the reordering/rebuilding of the Chapel by the Lady Richeldis after the Conquest, implying that the 'Lady of the Manor' was also termed Richeldis, which is also an appended name used for Edith Swanneshals, wife of Harold, who held the manor in 1066 and before. Clement V in 1306 sanctioned the appropriation by the Priory of the Church of St Peter Great Walsingham, the church to be served by one of the canons. Thus, the Church held lands in Great Walsingham, which were given to the church, probably prior to the Conquest as William held Walsingham from 1066, and there is no record of such a royal gift after that date. Therefore, the gift was probably made by the pre-conquest holders Harold and Edith or her half-brother Ketel, who also held lands in Walsingham. It is a reasonable assumption, therefore, based on the evidence above, that the date of 1061 is the date of the Shrine's foundation, as accepted by most commentators.

Notes

1 J. C. Dickinson, *The Shrine of Our Lady of Walsingham* (Cambridge: Cambridge University Press, 1956).

2 It is recorded in the Chronicles of 1063 and Charters dated to this period that it was during this campaign that Earl Harold was in north Wales in 1061–1063, acting with King Edward's warrant in doing battle against the Welsh prince; that Llewellyn was killed and, following the custom of this time, his sons were given ward of court status by Harold to prevent their death at the hands of the Welsh party who had traitorously slain their father. This has been misread or misunderstood as referring to Harold as the father of these two minors. There is evidence from the Chronicles 1064 that they were in their fourth and sixth years, and that Harold was in north Wales for a very limited period of five or six months, which makes it unlikely (in fact, impossible) that he married and sired two children of these ages. His campaign in Gwynedd took place in 1061–1063 and there is no record of a marriage of any kind other than *mores danico* to Edith the Fair. On p. 568, Stenton comments in the second edition of his work *Anglo Saxon England* that Harold was at the height of his powers at this time in the court of King Edward. It is not possible that a marriage to so important a person would go unrecorded by the Chronicles and Charters of this period. Following Harold's successes in Wales, he went to northern France on the famous diplomatic mission where he was shipwrecked and honoured, yet kept as a semi-captive by the Normans. This campaign makes it impossible for the unrecorded marriage to Princess Edith to have taken place.

3 Edith Swanneshals was clearly married to Harold Godwin, King of England; she is known as Edith or, as in the Domesday Book for Cambridge, Edeva Puella (surnames or familial names were not used in the eleventh century). The appended name 'Swanneshals' should not be translated as 'swan neck' but as fair and stately, graceful and elegant.

4 The reference is to land in Normandy titled Faverques and identified through the list of French sponsors of the second crusade, one of whom was the Bishop of Lisieux, for whom

a land-holding in nearby Lisieux in Normandy is referenced. Rychold Faverques is a Norman-French name and the land is probably in her or her family's ownership, thus enabling it to be entailed for the sum of 10 Marks as indicated in The Norfolk Roll 1130–1131. This entry refers to the founding of the Walsingham Priory Charter and also refers to a lady known as Rychold Faverches. This name implies that her and her family's wealth in part derives from a place called Faverches in Normandy, near the land of the Bishop of Lisieux who was a prominent sponsor and promoter of the second crusade. This name is not associated with 'Geoffrey', the tenant landholder in the late tenth century of the royal holding at Walsingham.

5 See University Library Cambridge, Ms.1i. Vi. 2.Fo. 71r. The folio is dated the fourteenth century and is sound evidence of a foundation date of the Shrine as 1061, as this Book of Hours from folio 73r has been copied, probably in a scriptorium, with no plausible reason to use a date other than that which is recorded and accepted as authentic at the time of writing. The dating evidence supports both the Pynson Ballad and the antiquarian John Leland in their dating of the Shrine.

6 Dickinson, *The Shrine*, p. 4.

7 See the cartulary, fo. 8r. = mon 73.

8 Dickinson, *The Shrine*, p. 5.

9 *Ibid.*, p. 6.

10 J. Leland, *Joannis Lelandi Antiquarii De Rebus Collectanea*, T. Hearne (ed.) (London, 1715), 17710, IV, 29.

11 There is no record in the Norfolk Rolls or the Chronicle records, the Domesday or the Charters which identify Geoffrey with the district of Faverches in Normandy where his assumed mother's entailed wealth was probably situated. There is also no recorded evidence of a blood-tie or any family association that shows any genealogies indicating a family name 'Faverches' that has come to light during my research.

12 Dickinson, *The Shrine*, Appendix D, figure XX, p. 174 (the St Laurence chapel). The figure shown is clearly of 'Old English' style in its arch construction.

13 Dickinson, *The Shrine*, Appendix D, p. 175.

14 *The Anglo Saxon Chronicles*, D. Whitelock (ed.) (London: Eyre and Spottiswode, 1961).

15 J. Lingard, *The Histories of Antiquities of the Anglo Saxon Church*, second edition (London: J. Booker Keating and Co., 1845).

16 This order of clerics was midway between a tonsured monk and the diocesan priest; they were ordered on the bishop but lived in a community that from early times was called a minster. They came to be known in the tenth, eleventh and twelfth centuries as Augustinian Canons because of the close ties with Augustine and his north African Cathedral community. They were also known in the tenth and eleventh centuries as Black Canons and Regular Clerks as well as Austin Canons.

17 This ancient order in its constitution as clerics as a cathedral or leading church community is the foundation in England of the old English minster or monastery, and provided a community base for clerics to administer to a wide area, which was necessary in partly-settled communities beyond the townships with a relatively small number of men ordered to the priesthood. They were the most widespread order in the second half of the first millennium of the Christian Church in the British Isles.

18 *Victoria County History, Norfolk*, vol. 2, W. Page (ed.) (London: Boydell & Brewer, 1906).

19 William de Warrenne was a considerable holder of land in Norfolk. *History of the Crusades*, vol. I, M. Bolin and K. Sutton (eds.) (Wisconsin: University of Wisconsin, 1919), pp. 474–478.

20 *History of the Crusades*, vol. I, M. Bolin and K. Sutton (eds.) (University of Wisconsin Press, 1919), pp. 474–478.

21 Dickinson, *The Shrine*, p 10.

22 *Ibid.*, p. 15.

23 Hervaeus, *Patrol.*, clxxxi, col. 140, as cited in E. Male, *The Gothic Image, Religious Art in France of the Thirteenth Century* (London: Collins, 1973), p. 165, n3.

24 Male, *The Gothic Image*, pp. 165–168. See also the work of C. R. Dodwell, *The Pictorial Arts of the West* (Yale: Yale University, 1993), pp. 800–1200. This work provides a very thorough critique of Mary as the Messianic lineage of Jesus.

25 The colouring, design and the form of the crowns on both Jesus and Mary are typically Anglo-Saxon.

26 *VCH Norfolk*, pp. 330–336. This record in the VCH implies at least that Edith the Fair was a favoured member of Edward's

court. We do not have a date for the listing of Edith Swanneshals as a royal patron, but it does establish her in her own right as a wealthy court member and patron of Cnut.

27 *Domesday Book,* P. Brown (ed.), general editor J. Morris (Chichester: Phillimore, 1984).

28 Dickinson, *The Shrine,* p. 4.

29 *VCH Norfolk,* pp. 394–401; Leland, *Collectanea,* iii, 26.

1

Historical Background

FROM THE LATE seventh century, for many decades (although not continuously), the central kingdom of Mercia, made up of the land between Northumbria and the Thames, together with Surrey, held a vacillating suzerainty over the entire southern peoples, including those in Kent and the East Angles, and the eastern and south-western Saxons. Only Wessex of old, divided into shires and sub-kingdoms, held out and resisted Mercian over-lordship. In 829, Egbert of Wessex took over the leadership of the English from the Mercians. Within 25 years of this date, Scandinavian Northmen invaded and settled in Britain, Ireland and northern France. They then settled and named their lands in France 'Normandy'. In England, they settled the territories known as the Danelaw: the lands east of the old Watling Street and the River Lea down to the Thames estuary, largely known today as East Anglia, and many other places. They based their armies on fortified boroughs which were supported economically by large areas of productive land adjacent to these strongholds. They were finally held in check within the boundaries of the Danelaw by Egbert's grandson, Alfred (871–899), and his son, Edmund (899–925), who also built and used these strategically located fortified boroughs. Edgar (959–975) was succeeded by his son, Aethelred II

(968–1016), who was threatened by a new invasion by the King of Denmark. Around 1008, the old kingdom of Mercia was reorganised along the ancient boundaries of the 'Hundred' and the Shire. However after much fighting and insurrection, including substantial bribes, the Danes prevailed. When Aethelred and his son Edmund Ironside both died in 1016 without heirs, the Danish King Canute became King of England and reigned until 1035. In his reign as *eorl,* the Saxon title became the Scandinavian *jarl,* the accepted title for regional rulers; in the early English period they were therefore referred to as 'aldermen.'

Canute appointed three great earls: Siward the Dane in Northumbria (the enemy of Macbeth); Leofric, a Mercian nobleman (husband of Lady Godiva), who died after 1066; and, south of the Thames, Godwin of Sussex, who married his sister-in-law or niece, Gytha. Godwin was succeeded by his second son, Harold, who died at the Battle of Hastings. When Canute died childless, Aethelred's son, Edward the Confessor (1042–1066), returned from exile in Normandy with his Norman companions to rule for twenty-four years.

Earl Godwin, supported by many powerful noblemen who were fearful of the King's Norman appointees, grew ever more powerful and restless and eventually the Earl and the noblemen were reconciled to Edward through marriage and preferment. King Edward married Godwin's daughter, Edith of Rutland. Godwin was succeeded in 1053 by his second son, Harold. In 1062, Harold's younger brothers, Gyrth and Leofwin, succeeded Leofric and Algar as the earls of Mercia and East Anglia. King Edward died on 5th January 1066 and Harold was immediately threatened by invasion from Norway and Normandy: although he defeated the Scandinavian armies at York, he was himself was defeated at the Battle of Hastings. William was crowned King at Westminster on Christmas Day 1066 and the Norman dynasty ruled, in place of the Anglo-Saxon line stretching back and beyond Alfred the Great.

The pride and self-understanding of the English was recorded by the nobility and clerical elite on their chronicled histories; that they were an independent nation with a unique history and were not part of some greater European empire, either French/Norman or Scandinavian. From 1066, until Henry III came to the throne, this independence from foreign suzerainty was breached; England was ruled by foreign dynasties following the Conquest. It was not until the reign of Henry III that independence as the British Isles was imposed by the House of Plantagenet. Up until the time of Richard, they were ruled as a sovereign region of northern Europe by a variety of Norman-French dukes and magnates, who were also titled kings of England. This Norman-French suzerainty that followed from William's conquest of England and the British Isles was a cause of resentment and hostility among the British and English nobility, who valued their linguistic and societal identity of an ancient island kingdom of disparate races that had become one nation. This social separateness from mainland and Scandinavian Europe, together with its indigenous wealth and its Christian identity, distinguished by the survival and ubiquity of the British language, was of great significance to the nation as an island race.[1]

Following a series of rebellions across the length and breadth of England, by 1084 the regional power bases of the English had been destroyed and the

Scandinavian-supported uprisings in East Anglia were also repelled by William, often with the assistance of north European mercenaries. The billeting and provision of these Norman armies revealed wide discrepancies in the tenure and value of land, manorial holdings and the tenancy rights of sub-tenants. Therefore, the due payment of the King's Tax revealed disputed rights and dues which were deemed the absolute right of the Norman King and his magnates. It also revealed the acquisition of land and property, and the usurpation of the just rights of many Englishmen and their families. This was one of the direct causes of the Domesday survey, which has a wealth of socio-economic data and is therefore a most valuable and unique historical document.

Many thousands of Englishmen who had held land freely were placed under Norman landholders, paying tax and levies on the productive capacity of their holding. This, then, was the aim of the Domesday Book: the King wanted to know what he had and who held it. Bishop Henry of Winchester added the wise corollary 'that every man should know his right and not usurp another's'. Therefore, in the Domesday Book, the first page of each county lists, in order of precedence, the principle landholders, headed by King William. Under each principle landholder is listed in the textual record 'who held the land before 1066 and who holds now'; in the Norfolk books, livestock is also listed, and this allows us to have a more detailed view of the intricate economic pattern and the socio-economic importance of manorial holdings in this area. The most important question of the Domesday survey was the first question listed, according to Morris, general editor of The Phillimore edition 1984: the name of the place, who held it before 1066, and now.[2] This will enable us to establish ownership in 1061 of the Walsingham Manorial Holding at the time of the foundation of the Shrine by 'The Lady of The Manor'. The term used in the LDB is *'Tempore Regis Edward'*, which may provide the evidence necessary to identify the person who asked 'Our Lady' for the honour of carrying out work on her behalf.[3]

We are seeking to identify the name and rank of the landholder of Walsingham Manor in 1061. King William is listed as holding *c.* 241 parcels of land in Norfolk; item 40 of the 241 described refers to Walsingham as follows:

> Harold held Walsingham before 1066, three caracute of land, that is (360) acres of productive land an outlier of the lands of Fakenham.
>
> Then and later 13 villagers now 6, then and later 7 smallholders now 5.
>
> Always one plough in Lordship, always 2 men's ploughs.
>
> Woodlands, 10 pigs, meadow one and half acres, 2 mills, Always 2 cobs, always five head of cattle, Then 12 pigs now 14. then 24 sheep, now 40.
>
> Also 9 Freemen at one caracute of land [this is calculated at 120 acres and may refer to a depot holding as a central point of deployment for The Lady of The Manor in erecting the House and its foundation Chapel]
>
> To this manor appertains 2 smallholders, meadow ½ acres, ½ mill. Then 3 ploughs, later and now 2 ploughs.
>
> All this is assessed in Fakenham.[4]

This manorial holding of Earl Harold, later King of England, is clearly of high value. On the death of his father in 1053, he was succeeded as Earl of East Anglia by his brother Ralph, but the irrefutable evidence of the LDB shows that he kept his holdings in Norfolk. These landholdings had come with his marriage to Edith, daughter of Wulfhilda, who on the death of her first husband had held these lands. There were in this compact manorial holding 720 acres of meadow, two cobs and, most economically important, two mills. In addition there were five head of cattle. Harold as earl would have had his manorial court in Walsingham, which is significant in terms of providing revenues from fines, duties and holding prisoners for the shire courts or the King's assize, where jurisdiction was held by the earl or sheriff directly officiating in the King's name. This manorial court still exists adjacent to the market centre of Walsingham, connected to the Priory grounds and manorial lands.

In addition, nine Freemen were a constituted body of skills over which the Lord and Lady of the Manor had jurisdiction. Walsingham in the North Greenhow hundred was only five miles north of Fakenham, which (as we see below) was the northernmost borough held by Harold, with considerable lands and income there from. They were termed and taxed as outliers with his own lands and tenement 'burgess' holdings providing him with a steady income.

These settlements were a vital part of the complex rural economies of the Danelaw. This town or borough was the place where Harold assembled much wealth and local power. In 1061, we can be reasonably sure that The Lady of Walsingham Manor was Harold's wife; that she was his sister, mother or daughter is unlikely and can be discounted on the following grounds. There is evidence that Harold's mother was residing in the Convent at Whitwell at this time and was domiciled at Winchester or with her eldest daughter Edith, who was to become wife of King Edward at the Courts in Winchester and London. Queen Edith was living at court, and Harold's other sister, Gytha, resided with her family in Mercia. His daughters were not yet of age and his wife Edith the Fair was very much alive and sometimes travelled to Waltham Abbey to be with Harold, her husband since 1042.

On this evidence, it is reasonable to conclude that The Lady of Walsingham Manor who was referred to as 'chief artificer' of the freemen who built Our Lady's Shrine of Walsingham was Edith the Fair and Rich (Rychold), the wife of Earl Harold. Harold would become chief advisor to King Edward, together with his sister, Edward's wife, Queen Edith.

This manorial holding of Earl Harold in Walsingham was part of a number of holdings in the hundreds of Greenhow (as set out in Appendix D), and was of high status adjacent to the holdings of King Edward. This is indicated by the requirement of six ploughs and its strategic proximity to both the sea and the King's own land holdings in North Greenhow. This manor was a compact high-status land-holding. Harold may have had his manorial court for the Hundred there in Walsingham when he was Earl of East Anglia.[5] When he became Earl of Wessex in 1053 on the death of his father, it was probable that the royal court in Fakenham became an Assize court; this was then Harold's focal point for regional jurisdiction as Earl of East Anglia prior to his father's death in 1052.

There is, then, some compelling evidence that the Lady of the Manor in 1061 was the wife of Earl Harold. Further contemporary evidence of Edith the Fair is found in the History of the Abbey of Saint Benedict at Holme. This lists donations to the Abbey, including that in 1046 given by 'Edgyoe Swanneshals'; these followed her earlier donations made under King Cnut (Edgyoe is an alternative rendering of Edith).

Edith also held the manor of Thurgaston in Norfolk. This is confirmed by a Charter of King Edward, reproduced in Dugdale's *Monasticum*, which refers to *'ecclesiam de Thurgatun cum tota villa'; this confirms the donation without giving the name of the donor.*[6] In the Norfolk Domesday, under the newly-termed High Sheriff Roger Bigot's land holdings (item 87 in the Hundred of North Erpinghan) Thurgaston is shown as a forfeiture now belonging to the king. It records in Thurgaston two smallholders belonging to the manor. The landholder before 1066 was Withri, who (with Ulfketel) was Harold's man. No reason is given for this forfeiture to the king of such a small and obscure land gift. The obvious explanation following its acceptance as a land gift related to Edith the Fair (wife of Harold) and 'his men' Ulfketel and Withri, is that it was part of the sequestration of all property and possessions of Harold Godwin's household and brothers at arms that would pass to the victor of the Battle of Hastings.

Professor Frank Barlow has suggested that Edith may have been the 'Ealdgyth' named in her mother's will and testament.[7] Wulfgyth's will is dated to 1042–53. This coincides with Edith the Fair's marriage to Earl Harold, who, in 1042/45 became Earl of East Anglia and in 1053 Earl of Wessex on the death of his father, Earl Godwin. This will bequeaths land at Stisted in

Essex to her sons, 'Aelfketel' (Ulfketel) and Ketel; land at Saxlingham and Somerton in Norfolk and Walsingham to her daughters, Gode and Bote; land at Chadacre, Suffolk. To her daughter Ealdgyth is bequeathed Ashford in Suffolk, and land at Fritton to Earl Godwin and Earl Harold. The Domesday Book confirms that land at Fritton was given to Earl Harold and Godwin, his father.[8]

These were probably dowry bequests, following a custom of gift-giving to very high-ranking and powerful magnates and their families on such occasions as marriage. This record supports the understanding that Edith the Fair was the daughter of Wulfhilda (also called Wulfgyth) and related through King Aethelred to King Edward as his niece.

In all probability, on the marriage of Wulfhilda's daughter Edith to Earl Harold, these gifts formed a pattern of land-holding beneficial to both families. Further, this marriage would probably have been conducted *mores danico,* as was the custom of both families whose marriages had been for centuries in like manner.

However, there is no evidence of such a marriage contract and both Edith and Harold were devout Christians (see Chapter 8); regarding Harold's great friendship with Bishop Wulfstan of Worcester, it is possible that a Christian marriage was celebrated. The changes confirming the Sacramental nature of Christian marriage had only recently been promulgated from Rome. Throughout the Danelaw and widespread among the nobility of England who now had many such Scandinavian bloodlines, the hand-fast marriage, which was customary and widely accepted throughout northern Europe, should not be referred to as an illegitimate union. We may recall that the English equivalent,

Common Law marriage, was recognised as law well into the nineteenth century. The following Domesday entry confirms this possible family allegiance of Wulfhilda's family and the Godwin dynasty. Listed under the new Norman patronage is the Land of Ralph of Beaufur, in the Walsham Hundred as follows:

Item 19

> In Woodbastick Godric, 1 free man held before 1066. 4 Freemen belonging in Wroxham, 7acres of land, 1 villager at 15 acres of land. Godric also held Tunstall before 1066. as a manor now Thorold holds, 60 acres. The jurisdiction is the King's. In Woodbastick Ulfketel and Withri, Harold's men, hold 4 Freemen and a half and 6 smallholders, 11 acres of land, meadow 1 acre; always ½ a plough.[9]

Here is first-hand evidence that Ulfketel was Harold's man, together with a man of possible Danish descent named Withri before 1066. Further to this, it is recorded in the Norfolk Domesday under the landholding of King William:

127

> In Saxlingham 1 free man under the patronage of Harold before 1066 held 30 acres of land.
>
> Always 3 smallholders, then 1 plough in Lordship, now ½.
>
> Also 1 Freeman 1 acre of land.[10]

Godric the Steward had custody of this land in the King's hand, but the land does not pay tribute to him. (Godric was the King's steward and acted 'in Livery', therefore he acted in the person for the King's Household and was not to be denied.)

This record underlines the close family ties of Earl Harold and his wife's relations, not merely through the family bequest of Wulfhilda. Once more, we have this evidence reinforced by this land-holding passing directly to the King as forfeited by the late King Harold, vanquished in battle. We also have an indication that is important in understanding the shorthand code used in the compilation of the LDB.

The freeman who held this land directly under Harold's patronage before 1066 is written in the lower case separately, denoting a man free from all encumbrances, including the freedom to go wherever he would and also to dispose of his land without hinder or permission as he pleased. Thus, such a man was under patronage and probably served his patron in some form, but his loyalty was through a personal bond of fealty without legal obligation, sometimes referred to as an honour code. Often in times of insurrection and warfare this entailed some form of military service, required formerly under the Middle English Thegn system of service and loyalty. This person was not necessarily a member of the noble classes and had, probably through personal service or mastery of a set of skills, achieved this status, which was curtailed under the Norman system of hierarchical land-holdings under the king, so that free men had rights of tenure and ownership or personal autonomy, subject to their immediate landholder. They were, then, no longer freemen under the new Norman regime. This was a major cause of resentment and in turn greatly reduced the value of minor land-holdings by imposition of some form of levy or rent, or some other form of tribute to which (in the Old English custom) they had not been subject previously. Under the new system, the Norman appointed owners could and did impose taxes that formerly had not been rendered. In contrast (and counterintuitively, in modern terminology), the upper case conjoined term 'Freemen' denotes a person who, although not tied to a certain place, was not free from specific lordship. Such persons were skilled artisans involved in many trades or mysteries. They were metalworkers, carpenters, hurdle-makers, slaughter-men, rough riders, millers, millwrights and wheelwrights etcetera. Thus they enjoyed within their community and hundred, borough or sometimes shire, freedom of movement necessary to carry out their trade. They were part of the manorial system within a defined locality and owed rent or some other form of dues or tribute to the Lord of the Manor. This class of freemen under patronage also included some clerks, as scribes to the various courts, and others with special skills, such as falconers, engineers, minor orders of the clergy and market traders, who had special permission from the manor or shire courts to move freely and enter into the purchase and sale of produce. There were also licensed 'moneyers' and officials in the service of the local magnates or the King. There were also 'riders'; these messengers would often hold their freedom in livery, that is directly from the King or earl; thus, we can glimpse, even in such a codified record as the Domesday Book, the diverse patterns of trade, commerce and social organisation of the English nation under Norman government in the eleventh century. The manorial system of jurisdiction within the hundred and the shire was essential, providing a base for local magnates, noblemen and landholders, closely identified and in the midst of the local agricultural productive centres, in order to control and preside over the local economy, the justice system. Social activity under the spiritual direction of the Christian church was also of importance in unifying the local regions into a nation.

This manorial system had developed through the centuries with the hundred and the shire, in part from the Anglo-Saxon custom of the Barton and the Royal Barton in conjunction with the travelling Court of the King. The Barton provided a centre of storage, maintenance and repair and provision as well as for the local community to assemble for all purposes and eventualities in a place suited for a large assembly of local people. It also provided a central means of transport for, and the slaughter and preservation of, livestock as well as a centre with the Great Barn for local gatherings and celebration of all kinds: for example, a place for holding the hundred, and on occasions the shire, courts.

These centres were for centuries the place of the hundred and kings' courts, presided over by the earl or someone designated, such as the shire reeve (or, in this case, the hundreds of South Greenhow or East Anglia). It could also be a place for the deliverance of tribute, food rent and the imprisonment of outlaws awaiting the King's Judgment and sentence. These places on a quarterly or annual basis gave hospitality to the King or his representative and his retinue of armed guards, clerks and noble retainers; very often these quarterly assizes were conducted and presided over by the great magnates acting for and on behalf of the King. These places, such as the Royal Barton at Bristol, near what is now the Fishponds area, developed into major settlements of towns or boroughs, situated very often on major rivers or the confluence of two rivers, such as the Avon and the Frome adjacent to towns and major highways. This basic plan of the regional city or town is evident today in the vast majority of shire towns such as Bedford, Bath, Gloucester and Worcester. These ancient settlements had also been exploited by the Romans during their occupation and settlement, and with a resident population occupying tenement holdings related to trade and commerce, they became ever more strategically important in the support of the great earls, who, in the early Anglo-Saxon period, presided over local or regional 'sub-kingdoms.'

It is against this historical development (with many local variations) that we come to understand the manorial system in place under Norman influence, and the changes that occurred in the eleventh century. An example of such a town or borough was Fakenham on the River Wensum, which linked it directly to Norwich and on to the port of Yarmouth. Fakenham is situated in a very favourable natural geographical locality. It commands the crossroads of ancient highways, running north to the coastal areas of the Wash, and south through Thetford and down to the Watling Street and the River Lea, the boundary of the Danelaw, leading through Waltham Cross to the Thames estuary and the great metropolis of London. Fakenham was five miles from the Old Saxon Cathedral settlement of Elmenham, replaced and removed to Norwich under the Norman ecclesiastical changes.

These highways of communication and transport also went west to Wisbech and Peterborough, east to the City of Norwich, and to the North Sea via Yarmouth. Fakenham is an ancient Anglo-Saxon settlement, and its name suggests a place of calm and cleansing: a wooded place for the chase. This place-name is a clear indication that it was used (perhaps even before the Romano-British period) as a pagan place of worship of the Goddess of Life and the associated water sprites. Early Romano-British Christian missionaries made use of such sites as holy places suitable for mass conversion involving the old baptismal rite of complete submersion in running water, just as John the Baptist carried out his mission of repentance in the Jordan. In the Domesday Book, it is described as two separate settlements on either side of the River Wensum: Fakenham and Hempstead.[11] 'Wensum' is a very ancient Old English river name, meaning wandering harmoniously, meandering gently and murmuring softly. The racecourse centre on the nearby heathland is probably referred to in the Wingate Old English Chronicle as a selling plate venue for unbroken colts. This centre of racing and breeding horses is another fact that adds credence to Fakenham as an Old English settlement of the eighth and ninth centuries, exploited by the tenth-century Danish armies in support of their fortified boroughs and mobile mounted squadrons of armoured militia.

Together with Hempstead, Fakenham at the time of the Domesday had a population (based on the values indicated in the LDB) in the order of 400 male persons, which equates to something in the order of 1,600 residents. Fakenham, at the time of Earl Harold, with his vast holdings in Norfolk alone and as a chief advisor to King Edward, together with his right of jurisdiction held from the Crown, with the Royal Court collecting fines, levy and tribute as well as administering the sale and distribution of goods and the King's coinage in the County, also provided prestige, great sources of wealth and, through Hempstead Priory, hospitality for many hundreds of officials, clerks, messengers, administrators and tax and other collectors and licensed purveyors of specialist goods and services. Inland waterways at this time were most important for the transport and distribution of farm implements and produce and luxury goods in bulk from other regions and places of importation. With much higher water tables, the depth and flow of these waterways was far greater than those of today. Flat-bottomed long boats, punts and rafts were much in use. Many of today's inland cities, such as Wisbech, Salisbury and many others, were major ports. All Harold's vast land-holdings in Norfolk were assessed in Fakenham and this gives a clear indication of the wealth and powers of civil administration that were handled in the borough of Fakenham before the Norman Conquest. This immense revenue and standing court together with the necessary administration was the base from which Harold governed. Five miles away in tranquil Walsingham, his Manor would surely have been a haven for his wife and family.

In our search for the identity of the person who was the Lady of The Manor of Walsingham in 1061, it seems that in all probability it was Edith the Fair, recorded as Edeva the Fair in the LDB of Cambridge set out below.

Edith Swanneshals was the wife of Earl Harold; they were married in *c.* 1042/5, in the very early years of the reign of King Edward the Confessor. There is no evidence available that can be traced as to the form of marriage, although second and third-hand sources were written by churchmen who, under political influence, were intent on denigrating King Harold's reputation, citing the Danish form of hand-fast marriage to imply at least an illegitimate union. It is clear from Bishop Wulfstan and the first-hand evidence of Canute's court that both Harold and Edith the Fair were devout Christians and were probably married by Archbishop Stigand or Archbishop Wulfstan. The evidence above is accumulated in various entries in the Norfolk Domesday book, the Will and Testament of Edith's mother Wulfhilda and the evidence of King Edward's charter with support from Dugdale's *Monasticum,* which all provide credence to the understanding of a regular and lawful union. Further to this is the record of family ties in gift lands, including those to Earl Godwin in 1042. Ulfketel, Wulfhilda's eldest son, together with Withri, is clearly identified as Harold's man and the family ties and land-holdings are indicative of close family bonds. We proceed now to examine the named landholders who, before 1066, held Great and Little Walsingham adjacent to and abutting onto Walsingham Manor, and which provide first-hand evidence of the nature and extent of these family connections.

21

Land of Reynold son of Ivo

Item 24. North Greenhow Hundred.

Ketel (with) one freeman, held Walsingham before 1066.

Always 19 smallholders, one plough, 2 caracute of land (240 acres).

Then 2 slaves now one.

> Meadow 2 acres. Then and now 2 ploughs in Lordship. Now 3. Woodland 8 pigs. 3 horses when he acquired it, 2 head of cattle now 1. Always 24 sheep. 24 Freemen appertain to this village. 60 and 10 acres of land, 2 smallholders, ½ mill. Then 3 ploughs when he acquired it and now 1 ½ ploughs. Value £6, now same.[12]

Ketel held the other Walsingham before 1066:

> 2 caracutes of land (240 acres).
>
> Always 4 villagers, then 21 smallholders now 18, always 2 slaves. Then 2 ploughs in Lordship. When he acquired it 1, now 2, men's ploughs, later 1, now 1 plough. Woodland 6 pigs, meadow, one acre, 1 mill.
>
> :-:
>
> 34. Land of Peter Valognes.
>
> Item 18. In Great Walsingham Humphrey holds 1½ caracute of land, 180 acres of which Bondi a Thane held. Always three villagers, 7 smallholders.
>
> 2 ploughs in Lordship meadow 4 acres then and later, 1 ½ men's ploughs now 1. Later 3 slaves now 4. Then 5 head of cattle now 1. Then 20 pigs now 25. Always 180 sheep Then 9 beehives now 5, Also 1 Freeman, 4 acres of land. Value then and later, 30s, now 40s.[13]

This land was delivered to make up a manor; his men do not know which. This Domesday record shows that, prior to 1066, Ketel held both Great and Little Walsingham, whereas the Manor of Walsingham is shown as in direct possession of King William, who took over the property from King Harold in 1066. The two adjacent village land holdings were held before 1066 by Ketel, the younger son of Wulfhilda and her first husband Ulfketel the Brave, and by his elder brother, Ulfketel, both of whom were kinsmen of Earl Harold. It may be argued that 'Ketel' was a fairly common name in these parts, and there is no sure proof of individual identity; however, when considered in the context of the cumulative data presented above, first-hand records provide sound evidence for the conclusion that Walsingham Manor in 1061 was not only in the possession of Earl Harold, but was a manorial holding set among his wife's family members' land-holdings, providing at the northern limits of the Danelaw a safe haven, together with his borough town of Fakenham, from where he convened the King's court as Earl of Wessex and advisor to King Edward.

It is evident that the Lady of the Manor of Walsingham, who, in 1061 carried through the building of a replica of the Holy House of Galilee at the command of Our Lady of the Salutation and Annunciation, was in all probability Edith, wife of Earl Harold. In support of the date of the foundation of the Shrine, we can now examine the document known as *The Pynson Ballad*. In the next chapter, we will begin by providing the reader with an historical essay setting out the events after the Shrine's possible foundation from 1061–1169, to the beginning of the reign of Henry II.

Notes

1 During the five hundred years preceding the Roman occupation, these islands had been settled around the coast and estuarine hinterlands extending inland along the many navigable rivers. The understanding of nationhood was alien to a disparate immigrant continental people, who were organised on a regional basis, ruled by a dominant overlord with many variations. In the south-west, a large proportion of the populace were summer migrants, hence the county name, Somerset, meaning 'a summer Settlement'.

2 *Domesday Book*, P. Brown (ed.), general editor J. Morris (Chichester: Phillimore, 1984).

3 *Domesday Book, Norfolk*, S. Morris (ed.) (Chichester: Phillimore, 1984), p. 113a (an outlier, lands of Fakenham).

4 *Domesday Book, Norfolk*, p. 113a (item 40).

5 According to the *VCH Norfolk* and the *VCH Northampton* (see R. A. Smith, 'Anglo-Saxon Remains', in W. Ryland, D. Adkins and R. M. Serjeantson, *A History of the County of Northampton* (London: Archibald, Constance and Co., 1902), coins of Edward the Confessor were struck at Dereham, and there are clear indications of a mint in his reign at Walsingham. This supports Walsingham Manor as a holding of Harold, sometime earl of East Anglia.

6 W. Dugdale and R. Dodsworth, *Monasticum Anglicanum: A History of the Abbies and other Monasteries, Hospitals, Friaries and Cathedral and Collegiate Churches, with their Dependencies, in England and Wales* (London: 1655).

7 F. Barlow, *Edward the Confessor* (London: Methuen, 1970), p. 28, footnote 4.

8 This 'Will and Testament' dated 1043–1053 includes land bequests to her sons Ulfketel and Ketel at Walsingham, East Carleton and East Harling in Norfolk, Saxlingham and Somerton. There are bequests to her daughters Bode and Gode and separately to Ealdgyth (Edith) and to Harold and his father Earl Godwin. See Appendix B, The Will of Wulfgyth.

9 *Domesday Book, Norfolk*, p. 228b (part two, item 19).

10 *Domesday Book, Norfolk*, p. 125 (part one, listed under William (land of), item 127).

[11] *Domesday Book, Norfolk,* p. 1 (part one, 1 free man, item 127).

[12] *Domesday Book, Norfolk,* p. 21 (part two, item 24).

[13] *Domesday Book, Norfolk,* p. 34 (part two, item 18).

2

The Shrine from 1061-1169

FOLLOWING THE DEATH of King Harold in 1066, the next twenty years was a period of insurrection and struggle for land and ownership, as the Norman conquerors appointed by King William consolidated their power and took over lands that had belonged to the vanquished nobility of the old Anglo-Saxon and Danish establishment. The Manor of Walsingham is recorded in the Norfolk Domesday book, just five years prior to the Battle of Hastings, passing (as shown above) from Harold into the ownership of King William. The villages of Great Walsingham and Little Walsingham adjoining this manorial holding, which had belonged to Ulfketel and his brother Ketel, were also under new ownership, and the Walsingham Manor, where now the Holy House of Nazareth was housed in the designated chapel, belonged to King William; new owners were in charge, although the Shrine so recently founded in the time of King Edward remained a local sign of Our Lady's grace. The brothers Ketel, Harold's men, would surely have fought (and may have died) with him at the battle of Hastings. The brothers of Harold Godwin fled to Ireland and eventually sought sanctuary in the Netherlands and Scandinavia. Harold's mother and elder sister moved to the safety of the convent in Winchester and Harold's wife Edith and (probably) two of their daughters fled to Denmark in 1076, as reported by Scandinavian *Skagrinda*. The shrine of Our Lady then passed into the hands of the King's appointed guardians and eventually into the care of Geoffrey. It seems that, given these circumstances, it is remarkable that the Shrine not only survived, but flourished quietly.

William left England in 1086 and died in France in 1087. His son, William Rufus, succeeded his father. He was crowned at Westminster in 1087 and died in 1100. By 1154, the Norman dynasty had ended with the reign of Henry I. In these troublesome years the Shrine of Our Lady, although in royal ownership, was not patronised by the nobility, but cherished and revered by the local populace, and especially by the people formed in the Danelaw community and the old Anglo-Saxon freedoms of greater autonomy of the individual. Their piety and loyalty remained with the old order of English practice of worship and sanctity at such sites where prayers were answered and the afflicted cured and symptoms relieved. The test of holiness was simple and widely understood: was suffering relieved; were cures effective and prayers answered? The proof of the effectiveness of the Shrine of Our Lady was the favours granted to the faithful. It was clear and simple, and they witnessed to these miracles: poor and rich, learned and unlettered, they came to offer their thanks to the Mother of God and to seek her help in their afflictions.

Lanfranc was appointed Archbishop of Canterbury by King William and was undoubtedly a king's man first and foremost. He established the primacy of Canterbury over York on the basis of a great deal of forged evidence, although it is probable that he was not aware of their fraudulent nature or the tainted sources of their production. It was in 1076 that Lanfranc, at his third council, carried through a comprehensive review of the English church. Pope Gregory VII had been elected three years earlier, and it was a favourable time to introduce and impose continental organisation and practices in the Old English church. Lanfranc was not wholeheartedly in favour of the imposition of all the Roman decrees, and he recognised that the ancient Church in England had much strength, and held fast to an orthodoxy that had been influenced by the ancient Eastern rites, for which he had great respect.

In the very difficult question of clerical celibacy, he was conciliatory, in that although he upheld the new canon law that all newly-ordained priests would be required to take binding vows of celibacy, he did not require that those who served in the married state to set aside their wives and families. In all parts of England, there were many old minster churches served by canons that were bound by vows of celibacy and this was a requirement of the Augustinian Canons from ancient times. The old English rural cathedrals were also moved to the new towns, and in Norfolk this meant, firstly, moving the bishop's cathedral from rural Elmenham to Thetford, under duress from the High Sheriff Bigot; and secondly, very soon afterwards, moving it again from Thetford to Norwich, before any cathedral had been built at Thetford.

However, the one aspect of English custom of which Lanfranc disapproved most strongly was the veneration given to local saints: mostly of English royal birth, their merits were (in his opinion) not proven. He was met with great opposition, even by the monks of his own cathedral. He only prevailed by decree, issuing a plain statement of his authority that would countenance no amelioration. The revised calendar of saints that he imposed omitted the names of many whose reputation for sanctity and intercession was most heartily believed in. Even so, he was forced by the weight of pious opposition to issue a calendar of local festivals that was not in any way influenced by continental preferment. He instead issued a calendar promulgated in the time of Edward the Confessor. These changes in church governance, and especially opposition to the old English order of saints and the sanctity of local shrines, prevailed through the time of the Norman dynasty until 1154 and beyond. Yet, in the midst of this upheaval and opposition, the Shrine of Our Lady of Walsingham flourished. By the time of his death, in 1089, Lanfranc had achieved great changes in the replacement of English bishops and abbots with Norman prelates, but clerical marriage continued for at least another two centuries, with benefices often passing from father to son as in the Eastern Orthodox church. The veneration of the old English saints revived and flourished under local patronage, and the ownership of parish churches by lay persons, such as Saint Peter's in Great Walsingham, was still widespread practice. It is therefore understandable that the Walsingham Shrine, for at least a century and a half following its foundation, is shrouded in obscurity as far as official court chronicler records are concerned.

During the reign of King William II until his death in 1100, the Shrine has no recorded royal reference, despite being owned by the crown. William's relationship with the church in England and on the continent was turbulent and fractious. Following Archbishop Lanfranc's death, he was very slow to appoint a successor until, when very ill, he appointed another Norman, Bishop Bec. On his recovery, he was opposed to all the Archbishop's wishes and was in total disrespect of all religious observance and lawful prerogatives. William II was also ruthless in his bitter relations with his brother, Robert. He sequestered and kept for himself the Archbishop of Canterbury's revenue and wealth by not appointing a successor: an effective way of making the wealth of the Church available to the Crown. He also used this administrative channel of additional funding for his own purposes in many parts of the country by failing to appoint any successors to vacant bishoprics. He was a flamboyant figure and never married; his father, despite his iron grip on Church affairs in England, was a very religious person.

William Rufus was neglectful of his religious duties and impatient and scornful of the many ceremonies which, as king, he was expected to attend and take a leading part in. He was in dispute with Lanfranc's saintly and popular successor, Archbishop Anselm, on a regular basis. These continual disagreements concerning church revenues and land-holdings and the appointment of bishops, abbots and senior clerics (who, as skilled administrators, he relied upon) were a cause of friction and an unseemly relationship between church and Crown during his lifetime, and had a negative impact on the identity of the founder of this popular local shrine, with its origins known to be from the time of the late English king Edward. William II died in a hunting accident when he was shot in the chest accidentally by one of his fellow huntsmen on 11 August 1100.

Henry I, known by his nickname, Henry 'Beauclerc', succeeded to the throne and reigned from 1100 to 1135.

Under his reign, relations between the Crown and church improved, and eventually Edward was raised to the altars as 'Confessor'. He was present at the time of his brother's death, and, acting with great speed and determination, he hastened to London. Three days later, he was crowned, although he was the youngest brother. The eldest brother, Robert, also claimed the English throne but was in Normandy at the time. Henry I, however, challenged his brother and won the decisive battle of Tinchebrai in 1106 in France. Robert was captured and imprisoned for the remaining 28 years of his life, which is a dreadful indictment of the character and overwhelming ambition of Henry. During his father's captivity, Robert's son, Clito, escaped and formed an alliance with Louis King of France, who reigned from 1108 to 1137. This made it inevitable that Henry I would be at war with the Duchy of Normandy through the years 1109-1120. William Clito died in 1128 and Henry completed the re-conquest of Normandy and returned the Duchy to the English throne. Henry's heirs, William and Richard, were both drowned in the White Ship in the Channel in 1120.

Henry's legitimate daughter, Matilda, who married firstly the German Emperor Henry V, and after his death Geoffrey, Count of Anjou in France, was in line to succeed. However, Stephen was crowned king and Matilda's claim was rejected. She nonetheless invaded England in 1137; this caused many years of civil war, and she only retired back to Normandy in 1147. Her husband, in the meantime, had conquered the Duchy of Normandy and when Stephen died in 1154, Henry II of Anjou succeeded to the English throne and reunited Normandy and England under his rule.

This sketch of English history, from the time of the death of the Conqueror in 1088 until the beginning of the reign of Henry II in 1154, is coincident with and the backdrop to the first ninety years of the existence of Our Lady's Shrine of the Salutation at Walsingham.

From the Norman through to the Angevin dynasties, until the time when the Shrine passed into the guardianship of the Augustinian Canons, it is evident that for many reasons the Shrine remained a place of local and regional pilgrimage endowed only with lands pertaining to the manorial holding of Harold, which passed into William the Conqueror's possession in 1066 until his death in 1087, and continuing in relative obscurity until the death of King John. Edith the Fair was close to King Edward, as evidenced by her patronage of Eastholm monastery; her mother was Edward's half-sister and the King's land-holding in North Greenhow was barely five miles distant from Walsingham. Edward was, therefore, probably very aware of the Shrine's foundation, thus the designation that it was founded during his reign in the year 1061. Through this period when England was part of a Norman empire and oft-times ruled from France (until the death of King John and reign of Henry III), the Shrine was without royal patronage.

It should be emphasised that the accusations which surfaced in Henry VII's reign of gullible and misinformed lay persons as ignorant innocents used for the furtherance of greater wealth and power, and of well-intentioned but ill-informed and uneducated clerics, is clearly and entirely refuted by the historical evidence of the foundation of the Shrine of Our Lady in Walsingham and its subsequent history. It was founded only five years before the nation was changed profoundly under Norman rule, uprooted through force of arms and resettled and reorganised administratively by a small band of foreign noblemen under a new monarchy. In addition, the new regime was opposed at the highest level of church governance to some of the old shrines and saints of Royal Anglo-Saxon England, which were abolished or demoted as places of prayer and petition, neglected and scorned; and yet many survive to this day. This disfavour of the Saxon Christian church was unfortunate and did not help the national standing of the Walsingham shrine.

Yet, despite this benign neglect and condescension, the hostility and the dismissal of such shrines as an example of antiquated ignorance, the pilgrims, the rich and the poor, the afflicted and the lame came to Our Lady for succour and were cured: all were comforted and renewed. At the end of the Angevin dynasty, after a hundred years of warfare, the death of at least four kings and thousands of their followers, there remained in Norfolk this gift of grace: the presence of Our Lady and the work and inspiration of one woman, Edith the Fair, wife of King Harold, respected matron and mother, in whose honour this book is written, the Lady of the Manor who asked that she should do some work for the Mother of God.

In parochial, beautiful Norfolk, far from the great and the powerful, our most highly-favoured Lady, Mary the Mother of God, reigns in this England, Her Dowry, in Her Holy House of Nazareth where the Archangel Gabriel saluted Her from Heaven and announced the birth of Our Lord Jesus Christ. This is a woman's story: let all men tell of it and marvel at these mighty deeds of peace and healing.

3

The Pynson Ballad

THE INITIAL DESCRIPTIVE narrative recording the foundation in 1061 of the Walsingham Shrine is embedded in the sixteen-verse ballad, printed possibly in the late 1490s, but probably thirty years earlier. In verses three, four and five, there is an ancient detailed account of the foundation history of the Walsingham Shrine. The ten verses that follow, numbered six to sixteen, are a narrative version which follows a retrospective analysis and partial historical review, addressed to an audience of readers and listeners beyond the local and Anglo-ecclesiastical audience, with the final five sections composed as an exhortation or rousing preamble to encourage prayerful preparation before a visitation to this, Our Lady's place of healing.

The ballad was first printed in various editions of the records of the Shrine: this is apparent when we examine the texts in verses three, four and five and subject them to a comparative analysis with the opening two verses of the ballad. Based on the life and known chronology of the printer, Richard Pynson, it was published in the latter part of the reign of Henry VII. Pynson became publisher to the King in or about 1506 and the Pynson Ballad was one of his first commissions, which he carried out probably before his Royal appointment was confirmed. Henry VII died in 1509 and was succeeded by his son, Henry VIII, who retained Pynson as Royal Printer. Pynson was involved in many varying projects, including later with John Leland, who, as the King's Antiquarian was charged with the preservation and recording of the historical records of abbeys, colleges and schools, which were being sold or lost as a result of the dissolution and decline of the monasteries. This educational and very important historical legacy was a source of detailed documentation, which Henry VIII commanded should be preserved.[1]

Pynson was born in 1448 in Normandy, which included some territories over which Henry VII had a greater measure of control than his successor, Henry VIII. This was part of the much-disputed legacy of William the Conqueror. Henry VII, who had gained the throne of England following his invasion from exile in Brittany, was very much at home in northern France, with which there were at this time innumerable trade links, and of course many family ties with the English nobility. Pynson began his printing career in London in 1492 having served his apprenticeship and set up as a master printer; this was the year in which he printed Alexander Grammaticus's Doctrinal in London.

During this initial period he probably worked in Saint Clement Danes, outside Temple Bar. He became the King's Printer to Henry VII in 1506. This office carried with it not only great prestige, but also an annularly of two pounds (later doubled). This was a lifetime appointment and reflected the importance of his work for the Royal Court. He was acknowledged for his expertise in printing law texts such as, the statutes of the King. He also printed high-standard religious works, such as missals, books of hours and other devotional manuals, all of which required meticulous accuracy and quality presentation. As the King's Printer, his most famous historical work was *Assertio septem sacramentorum adversus Martinum Lutherumin 1521*, a consequence of which was that King Henry VIII was given the Papal Title of *Defensor Fidei*.[2]

As printer to the King, with a reputation for quality and accuracy, and working for a very critical and powerful readership, we can place great store on this printed edition of the Pynson Ballad. It was commissioned very early by Henry VII in Pynson's professional life as a printer and was therefore probably instrumental in his confirmation as Royal Printer to the King. We therefore must take care in our understanding and critique of the text therein, which further underlines the fact that we are considering four hundred years of royal ownership from this time in the 1490s, of the Shrine dated by 'The Chroniclers' as 1061.

The Ballad we have today has sixteen verses. It is a compilation of versification, some of which in its use of Late Old English in its descriptive narrative corroborates a date of composition in the first half of the eleventh century under King William, but openly loyal to his predecessor Edward. However, this use of a Late English written vocabulary is complemented by a romantic Norman-French series of verse using such expressions as *sauns fayle* and *inconuentyente;* the spelling is idiosyncratic throughout, but the use of contrapuntal repetitious rhyming is a clear echo of the Classic Latinised balladeering tradition. Considered overall and comparing it with the very limited documentation of the period, it is clearly of the early

Norman era. This document combines latinised Norman French with Late English verse and spelling, but has none of the tortured spelling, vocabulary and syntax of Middle or Early Latinised English. This additional internal evidence indicates that it was compiled from various sources in the early Norman era. It is, in summary, a High Norman-French manuscript compiled from at least three different sources, derived from an oral Late English tradition. It is preserved in part within a local oral tradition, where the intimate detail of the site's construction is set out and later written down. This balladeering was sometimes accompanied on a string instrument, probably a kind of contemporary lute. This was probably used as a prompt and *aide mémoire* and functioned as part of the wider dispersed 'Chronicles'.

Throughout the Norman era and on to the Tudor period, the ballad was the medium by which the great and good news stories of the day were broadcast. These dramatic stories were proclaimed in castles, baronial halls and manorial courts throughout Christendom. Wherever there were places of public assembly, the balladeer came forth to tell his tale. Battles were relived, great deeds recalled and the comical events and tragedies of human life re-enacted, including romances and the lives of heroes. In the towns, cities, cathedrals and monasteries the life of the people was celebrated: famine, fire, pestilence and miraculous events were dramatized and sometimes re-enacted. The drama of the seasons and the annual Christian liturgy was brought before the audience to edify and uplift them. From time immemorial, people had gathered to listen to the storytellers, the balladeers and the important royal or baronial proclamations. On high days and holydays, the mummers acted out these stories in a stylised version that could be understood by those who only spoke and understood the local dialect.

We understand, then, that the Pynson Ballad was the celebrated and cherished history of what became one of the most famous shrines in the whole of Europe. The detailed events of its founding with the full involvement of the local population and the very detailed foundation story were retold; the afflicted were cured; a great many were moved to repentance and prayer; the poor given relief and the sick cured. It was where prayers were answered and Jesus adored; this was confirmation of a Loving God. Here was a Holy place of prayer, praise, petition and cure, a good news story that all people of goodwill wanted to hear.

The Shrine of Walsingham, so the Ballad relates in verse three, was the work of 'a noble widow', sometime Lady of this town, called Rychold, in living 'full virtuous'.[3] The name Rychold is, then, a name of honour, given out of respect for her reputation as a virtuous woman. In the ballad, she asks whether she can (in gratitude for former prayers answered) be given some task or bestow some gift as an act of thanksgiving in honour of Our Lady.

The name Rychold means rich in the sense of 'fullness' or 'full of', in that it implies a whole person who lives fully a life of virtue. The final line of this verse is 'unto her worschyp to edefye this chapel'; the archaic meaning of worship is worthiness or merit, recognition due to someone out of honour or respect. 'To edefye' here is taken from the Old French, meaning to build and organise a complex structure. 'Chapel' here is Middle English, taken from Old French deriving from Medieval Latin, 'cappella' from 'cappa' meaning 'cloak' (the first chapel was a sanctuary in which Saint Martin's cloak was preserved). The Holy House was therefore built to be housed in honour of the salutation of Mary in a chapel where it was preserved, the work of human hands for the veneration of the faithful. 'The Lady of this Town' is described as a widow who no longer resides in Walsingham; this of course would be historically correct if we accept that the Lady of the Manor was Edith, the wife of Earl Harold in 1061 and the dead King of England by 1066. This would date the ballad as written after 1066, which, as shown below, is supported by the historical chronology of these events. In 1061, Earl Harold recovered from some form of paralysis and he, with his wife Edith the Fair, offered thanks to God for the intercession of Saint Laurence, whose chapel at Waltham and Walsingham was a private place of family worship. To give thanks for this cure and Harold's recovery may have been the event for which his wife was making her offering to Mary. This was normal practice in return for a request granted in Christian England in the medieval era. The work may have been the founding of a hospital for the poor and sick, the provision of a chapel or church for the remote parishes, or the endowment of some order or monastic institution. These endowments were widespread and supported the widowed, the poor, the destitute, the orphaned, the sick, pilgrims and other travellers and any in distress. They were inspired by grateful supplicants, who desired to carry out the work of Jesus the Christ in the time of their exile here on earth.

In the year 1061, since Our Lord's Incarnation, the noble Lady of Walsingham was given a vision of The House of Nazareth where the Angel Gabriel first saluted Our Lady and announced that Mary would be The Mother of God. The Lady of Walsingham was commanded to build an exact replica of the house in the grounds of the Manor of Walsingham and house it in a chapel for its preservation. It is notable that, just like the Shrine of Our Lady at Lourdes and the Shrine at Knock in Ireland, the visionaries avoided all personal fame and notoriety for themselves. The only focus of attention was and ever would be the work of Our Lady. However, wherever the individual visionaries are known they are accorded great respect and honour and some with beatification. In the year 2061, it will be a thousand years since Our Lady honoured the Lady of Walsingham with the vision of the Holy House of Nazareth. Yet we know nothing of this Lady except the honorific title Rychold. Therefore, we begin our search with this personal appellate title that means rich or highly-favoured. It is a title given to Mary the Mother of God and taken from the Gospel of Luke 1:26-38. 'Highly-Favoured Lady' is a reference to the Angelic events of the Salutation and Annunciation and also an honorific referring to the Visionary herself. The extant contemporary records of English, Norman-French and Danish nobility have no mention of such names, except that the name 'Edith' bears the meaning rich. It is therefore clear that it is not a personal or family name, and it was not the custom to refer to persons at this time by a Christian name affixed to a surname. The identity of the Lady of Walsingham has been hidden under the protective cloak of Mary the Mother of God, that most highly-favoured of all women. The evidence as shown above (taken from the LDB dated 1086) indicates that Rychold was probably Edith the Fair, the wife of Harold II, King of England.[4]

However, it is the name in its Latin form, 'Edeva', in the Somerset and Cambridge Domesday books, together with the appellation 'Puella', which reads as Edith the Young and Fair, that supports the understanding that the title Richeldis is a Norman-French translation of the Lady of the Manor in an English form of Rich and Fair.[5] Thus we have this name in use at this date of 1088, referring to a date prior to 1066 as the same named Edith, wife of Earl (and later King) Harold. This is most important in the cumulative evidence that, to my mind, confirms that the Visionary of Walsingham was most probably Edith the Fair, wife of Earl Harold, married in the reign of Edward the Confessor *c.* 1042-1045. This range of dates is compatible with the known dates of Edward's reign and the age range of the family of Harold and Edith.

The following is a modern printed version of the Pynson Ballad, set out verse by verse with the author's transliteration offset immediately below each verse, together, where necessary, with a discussion of the meaning. This printed account of the Walsingham Shrine's Foundation was a Royal commission of great importance to our understanding of the identity of the visionary lady, through whose labours and devout prayers the Royal Shrine adorns the Christian Kingdom of England: Mary's Dowry. This unique Shrine has as its foundation the Chapel, wherein the replica of the Holy House of Nazareth is housed, in memory of the saving events of the birth of Jesus.

It is a detailed account of the human response to the Visionary's instructions, which were clearly beyond the knowledge and skills of the human artificers. The Visionary is referred to by the soubriquet Rychold, which in the context of the verse apparently means rich and honoured, as well as the plain meaning of having riches of wealth, beauty or dignity. Her identity as Lady of the Manor of Walsingham is without further explanation; yet clearly after the 1066 conquest the Manor became a holding of King William and this implies a foundation prior to the year of William's Coronation. William was a devout man and clearly did not give this holding to a powerful magnate of the French invasion force under his command; rather it is clearly titled in the LDB of Norfolk completed in 1086, as the 'LAND of the KING'.[6] It was, therefore, a Norman Royal acquisition, and was left undisturbed, either by neglect or as a deliberate act of respect to King Edward. With regard to the Shrine chapel that had only recently been built as a private chapel, this remained in private ownership under royal patronage. Or most probably it was a public reminder of the reign of King Edward and thereby protected under William's accession to the English throne as conferred by King Edward. In the view of the Conqueror, he was the legitimate successor according to the Norman account of the right to the privy possession of Edward the late King of England. This claim confirmed the legitimacy of William's conquest and succession and therefore the royal ecclesiastic foundations such as the Walsingham Shrine went unmolested. However, this shrine, so closely associated with Harold's wife, was not promoted, and benign neglect ensured that there would be no association that would have promoted Harold as a Christian magnate, thus making possible his surviving sons' legitimate threat to the Norman succession.

The Pynson Ballad

Verse 1

Of this chapel se here the fundacyon,
Bylded the yere of crystes incarnacyon,
A thousande complete syxty and one,
The tyme of sent Edward Kyng of this region

Of this chapel see here the foundation,
Built in the year of Christ's Incarnation,
A thousand complete sixty and one years
In the time of St Edward, King of this region

The reference to the king as 'sent' or saint is worth comment, because his official date of canonisation is 1161. However, for over a thousand years English saints were sanctioned by public acclaim and this was only regularised as a Roman prerogative at the end of the eleventh century. The Ballad, promoting the shrine and using a lower-case spelling, does not undermine the Shrines' foundation date of 1061; rather, it supports the understanding of Edward's saintly character and reputation during his lifetime. There is in this verse the word 'region' rather than county or land, which provides an indication that this ballad was glossed or compiled by a Norman-French hand before its printing in France by Pynson in the time of Henry VII, when his realm would have included only minor holdings in northern France; therefore, the use of this term 'region' indicates a composition by an author in the Norman/Angevin era when England was indeed held to be a region of the Norman empire. This verse also stands alone and was clearly composed and affixed later than verses describing the actual events of the Shrine's foundation. It proclaims the date of the foundation in absolute terms and gives Royal approval to this most venerated of shrines, as well as its foundation date.

Henry VII had no practical reason for changing or supporting this dating of the Shrine, which adds veracity to the 1061 dating. Henry Tudor did not need to acquire a lineage of direct ancestry to Edward the Confessor, and the Walsingham Shrine had no bearing on his claim to the throne. His interest was the result of his three-day pilgrimage to the Shrine prior to his victory at the battle of Stoke. It was also a royal foundation, and he conjectured that, as such, any appointments in relation to the Shrine were a Royal prerogative. The Augustinian guardians were able to show that all such appointments since the first Charter were made without royal approval. The archaic spelling and vocabulary in the introductory verse also support an early dating of local English origin, as it does not bear the Norman-French clerical construction with its Late English spelling and syntax.

Verse 2

Beholde and se, ye goostly folks all,
Which to this place have devocyon,
When ye to our Lady askynge socoure call
Desyrynge here hir helpe in your trybulacyon
Of this hir chapel ye may se the fundacyon
If ye will this table overse and rede
Howe by myracle it was founded indede

Come and see, all you devout peoples
Which to this place have devotion,
When you ask Our Lady for succour
Desiring her help in your tribulation
Of this her chapel you may see the foundation

Turn over this tablet and read
How by miracle it was founded indeed

These opening verses lead us into what is clearly the story of the founding of the Shrine held in memory by those local artisans and villagers involved in the work of erecting the Holy House under the guidance and instruction of the Lady of the Manor. This communal memory plays a vital role in any oral tradition where the historical events were enacted in the presence of those who knew the facts at first-hand. This oral tradition would have been retained within the local community for at least three generations, spanning over a hundred years. It probably maintained the tradition in its purest form and would act to reduce error and exaggeration and embellishment, to maintain a true record and understanding of these stupendous events. We will show later that the Walsingham Shrine, in the first century of its existence, was supported by (and grew out of this local devotion in) the county of Norfolk. For at least 120 years, the Holy Shrine was not richly endowed or patronised by kings and nobles; its fame grew from favours granted to the sick and poor and miracles of healing attested by the pilgrims and the faithful. This is not the place to carry through a detailed critique and appraisal of this historical veneration of the Shrine: such a work is for a more devotional purpose and for some other project.

Verse 3

A noble widowe somtyme lady of this towne,
Called Rychold in lyvynge full vertous
Desyred of Oure Lady a petycyowne
Hir to honoure with some werke bountyous
This blyssed Virgin and Lady most gracious

Graunted hir petycyon, as I shall after tell,
Unto hir worschyp to edefye this chapel

A noble widow, sometime lady of this town,
Called Rychold, in living full virtuous,
Desired of Our Lady a petition,
To do her honour, with some bounteous work
The Blessed Virgin and Lady most gracious
Granted her petition, as I will recount,
To build this chapel unto Her worship

The honorific appellation Rychold has cognate meanings of splendid or costly. Rychold has also a Latin root from 'Rex' (king); this is reinforced from the Middle English/Old French *riche;* it also has a connotation from the Germanic of power together with authority. This reference to the Lady of this Manor as a widow supports a date of composition after the death of Harold in 1066. This understanding confirms a date for the ballad's historical foundation as probably written in the late Norman period or in early 1090 to 1150 in the Angevin dynasties, when the Shrine was held in private from the King. If we compare the vocabulary and syntax of the Austin Friars' cartularies to these verses, it is apparent they were composed and written by several hands schooled in a different tradition.

Verse 4

In spyryt Our Lady to Nazareth hir led
And shewed hir the place where Gabryel hir grette:
"Lo, daughter consyder," to hir Oure Lady sayde,
"Of thys place tale thou suerly the mette,
Another lyke thys at Walsyngham thou sette,
Unto my laude and singular honoure;
All that me seke there shall find socoure.

In spirit, Our Lady led her to Nazareth
And showed her the place where Gabriel had greeted her:
"Lo, daughter, consider", to her Our Lady said,
"Of this place take thou surely the measurement
Another like this at Walsingham you should set down
Do this in my praise and honour;
All that seek me there shall find succour.

Verses 5 & 6

"Where shall be hadde in a memoryall,
The great joy of my salutacyon.
Fyrste of my joys grounde and orygynal
Rote of mankynds gracious redempcyon
When Gabryell gave me relacyon
To be a moder through humylyte,
And goddys sonne conceyve in virgynyte."

"Where shall be built a memorial
Recalling the great joy of my Salutation,
First of my joy's ground and original
Root of mankind's gracious redemption,
When Gabriel related to me that I would
Be a mother through humility,
And God's son conceive in virginity."

This vysyon shewed thryse to this devout woman
In mynde she marked both length and brede;
She was full gladde and thanked Oure Lady than
Of hir great grace never destytute in need.
This forsayde hous in haste she thought to spede,
Called to hir artycyfers full wyse
This chapel to forge as Our Lady dyd devyse.

This vision was shown three times to this devout woman
In mind she marked both length and breadth.
Full of gladness she thanked Our Lady,
For her great grace that never fails those in need.

This aforesaid house she hurried to have built,
She called to her freemen artificers full wise
This chapel to forge, as Our Lady did devise.

Verses 7 & 8

All this a medewe wet with dropes celestyall.
And with sylver dewe sent from on hye adowne
Excepte tho tweyne plaves chosen above all
Where neyther moyster ne dewe myght be fowne.
This was the first pronostycacowne,
Howe this our newe Nazareth shold stande,
Bylded lyke the first in the Holy Lande.

When it was al fourmed than had she great doute
Where it shod be sette and in what maner place,
In as muche as tweyne places were founde oute
Tokened with myracle of Our Ladyes grace
That is to say, tweyne quadrates of egall space,
As the flees of Gideon in the wet being drye,
Assynged by myracle of holy mayde Mary.

All this should be done in a meadow wet with drops celestial.
And with silver dew sent down from on high
Except those two[7] *places chosen above all*
Where neither moisture nor dew might be found.
This was the first prognostication of
How this our new Nazareth should stand,
Built like the first in the Holy Land.

When it was all formed, then she had great doubt
Where it should be set and in what manner of place,[8]
In as much as two places were found
Indicated with [the] miracle of Our Lady's grace,
That is to say twin quadrates of equal space.
As the fleece of Gideon in the wet being dry,
Shown by a miracle of the Holy Maid Mary.

The Story of Gideon (Judges 6:36–39)

The sign of the fleece

If it is really you delivering Israel by means of me, as you have said, look, I am going to put a woollen fleece upon the threshing floor; if there is dew only on the fleece and all the ground stay dry, then I shall know that you will deliver Israel by means of me, as you have said. And so it happened. Early next morning Gideon got up, squeezed the fleece and wrung out enough dew to fill a cup. Gideon then said to God do not be angry with me if I speak once more, just once more, let the fleece alone be dry and there be dew all over the ground. And God did so that night. The fleece alone stayed dry and there was dew over all the ground.

This biblical reference confirms the detailed understanding of the Old Testament in the English Medieval church. It also confirms that the book of Judges was a model for the understanding of the role of rulers in Christian lands, as opposed to the late and mistaken assumption that Christian rule was only known in the sense of absolute monarchical hierarchies, which of course is a Norman legacy. The autonomy of the political role of judges in the Old Testament in relation to the anointed King, as part of the role of the prophetic movement as a constraint upon the King's misuse of his personal power and authority, was part of the ancient Anglo-Saxon culture of the anointing of kings in the manner of King David, who was subject to prophetic denunciation and sanction by Nahum. It is epitomised in the confrontation of Nahum and King David over his misuse of his authority to marry Bathsheba, in conspiring in the death of her husband, by ordering him to the front rank of battle where his demise would be almost certain. This indicates a possible Anglo-Saxon source in the scribal influence of the author of the ballad.

Verse 9

The widowe thought it most lykly of congruence
This house on the first soyle to bylde and arere
Of this who lyst to have experience
A chapell of saynt Laurence standeth nowe there
Faste by tweyne wells, experyence doth thus lere,
There she thought to have set this chapell
Which was begonne by Our Ladyes counsell.

The widow thought it most likely and agreed
This house on the first soil to build and erect
By those who wish to enquire
A chapel of St Laurence now stands there
Fast by two walls, enquiry does teach
There she thought to have set this chapel
Which was begun by Our Lady's counsel

This matter reveals a difference of opinion between the artisan freemen and the Lady of the Manor, which was resolved through the intercession of Our Lady supporting the knowledge and experience of the local builders. It also confirms that the local people, led by the artisans or skilled workmen, were highly involved in this communal work of building the Holy House of Nazareth in Walsingham. Although by 1066 it was a Royal holding and remains so to this day, it was from the beginning an Anglo-Saxon shrine which grew in faith and piety and general fame from the devotion and dedication of the local English community. The Roman hierarchy and the Norman Conquerors failed through the centuries to fully grasp and engage in understanding with the great loyalty and faith of the

English Church brought to these shores by the Roman armies and the orient traders, such as Joseph of Arimathea and many others, who according to legend and the written and archaeological evidence came to these shores many centuries prior to the Roman conquest.

Verses 10 & 11

The carpenters began to set the fundamente
This hevenly house to arere up on hye,
But sone their werkes shewed inconvenyente.
For no pece with oder wolde agre with geometrye;
Than were they all sory and full of agonye
That they could nat ken neither mesure ne marke
To ioyne togyder their owne proper werke.

They went to reste and layde all thynge on syde,
As they on their maystresse had a commaundement;
She thought Our Lady, that fyrste was hir gyde,
Wold convey this worke aftyr hir owne entent;
Hir meyny to reste as for that nyght she sente
And prayed Our Lady with devoute exclamacyon,
And as she had begonne, to perfowrme that habytacion.

The carpenters began to set the foundations
In order to erect this heavenly house up on high
But soon their work became troublesome
For no piece with another would agree with geometry;
Then were they all sorry and full of agony
That they could not understand measure nor mark
To join together their own proper work.

They went to rest and laid all things to one side,
As they on their mistress had a commandment
She thought Our Lady, that first was her guide
Would convey this work after Her own intent;

Her household rested for the night
And she prayed to Our Lady with devout exclamation,
And as she had begun, to perform that habitation.

Verses 12 & 13

All nyghte the widow remaynyng in this prayer
Oure blyssed Ladye with hevenly mynystrys
Hirsylfe being here cheyf artyfycer,
Arerid this said hous with aungelly's handys
And nar only reyrd it but set it there it is
That is, two hundred fote, and more in dystaunce
From the Fyrste place bokes make remembraunce.

Erly when the artyfycers cam to their travayl
Of this sayd chapell to have made an ende,
They founde eche parte conjoined sauns fayle
Better than they coude conceyve it in mynde;
Thus eche man home agayne dyd wynde,
And this holy matrone[9] thanked Oure Lady
Of hir great grace shewyd here specially.

All night the widow remained in prayer
Before our Blessed Lady with heavenly ministrations
Being herself the chief artificer,
Erected this house with angel's hands,
And not only raised it but set it where it is,
That is, two hundred feet or more in distance,
From the first place folks make remembrance.

Early when the artificers came to their work
Of this chapel to have made an end
They found each part fitted without fault
Better than they could imagine
Thus each man again went home
And this Holy Matron thanked Our Lady
For Her great grace, showed here specially.

Verse 14

And syth here Our Lady hath shewyd many myracle,
Innumerable, nowe here for to express
To suche as visyte thys hir habytacle,
Ever lyke newe to them that call hir in dystresse.
Foure hundredth yere and more to cronacle to witness
Hath endured this notable pylgrymage,
Where grace is daily shewyd to man of every age

And ever since Our Lady has shown many miracles here,
Innumerable, too many to be expressed here
To such as visit this her abode,
Ever like new to them that call her in distress.
Four hundred years and more so the chronicle gives witness,
Hath endured this notable pilgrimage,
Where grace is daily showed to man of every age

The printed version of the Pynson Ballad I date to *c.* 1490, as above, and this verse also underlines the reference to the Royal Chronicle recording events and miracles granted to the pilgrims to Walsingham for over four hundred years, indicating a range of dates from *c.* 1490 onwards, and thus providing a range of dates for the printing and distribution of this edition. This dateline is confirmed by my analysis above of the linguistic sources and style of composition, and confirms the antiquity and authorial sources from or immediately following the Conqueror's departure from England.

Verses 15 & 16

Many seke ben here cured by Our Ladyes myghte
Dede agayn revyved, of this is no dought,
Lame mayd hole and blynde restored to syghte
Maryners vexed with tempest safe to porte brought

Defe, wounded and lunatyke, that hyder have sought
And also lepers here recovered have be
By Oure Ladyes grace of their infyrmyte

Folkes that of fiends have had acombraunce
And of wicked sprytes also moche vexacyon
Have here be delyvered from every such chaunce,
And soules greatly vexed with every tempacyon
Lo, here the chyef solace against all trybulacyon
To all who seek bodely or goostly,[10]
Callynge to Our Lady devoutly

Many sick have been cured by Our Lady's might
Dead again revived, of this there is no doubt,
Lame made whole and blind restored to sight,
Mariners vexed with tempest brought safely home to port,
The deaf, wounded and lunatics that hither have sought
And also lepers have been recovered here,
By Our Lady's grace, of their infirmities.

Folk that have been possessed by demons
And of wicked spirits had also much vexation,
Have here been delivered from every such chance,
And souls greatly vexed with every temptation,
Lo, here the chief solace against all tribulation
To all who seek, boldly and devout,
Call on Our Lady devoutly.

Verses 17 & 18

Therefor every pylgrym gyve your attendaunce
Our Ladye here to serve with humble affecyon.
Your sylfe ye applye to do hir pleasuance.
Rememberynge the great joye of hir Annuncyacyon
Therewith concevyng this brief complacyon
Though it halte in meter and eloquence.
It is here wryten to do hir reverence

All lettered that wyll have more intelligence
Of the fundacyon of this chapel here,
If you wyll ask bokes shall you encence
More clerely to undersclnde this forsayd matere;
To you shall declare the cronyclere
All cyrcumstaunce by a noble processe
Howe olde cronyclers of thys bere wytnesse.

Therefore every pilgrim offering attendance,
To serve Our Lady with humble affection,
You bring yourself to do her pleasure,
Remembering the great joy of her Annunciation.
Herewith understand this brief compilation,
Though it falters in metre and eloquence
It is written to do her reverence

All men of letters, who have more intelligence
Of the foundation of the chapel here,
If you will consult folks you may encounter
We may more clearly understand this matter.
Then you in turn can declare it to the Chronicler
All circumstances by a noble process
To this old chroniclers bear witness.

It is of note that there is in this document, commissioned by King Henry VII, specific reference to the Chronicler. This, as is well known, is an official record of events of dynastic and regional interest generally circulated within court circles regarding matters of importance in the realm and its trade and social relationships with other kingdoms. Its reach as a source of news officially sanctioned by the Royal court was international. This record of historical events is a fundamental source of great importance and, though not absolutely free of bias or error, does give credence to the Walsingham Shrine and its importance and popularity throughout the realm and beyond. The Chronicles are a very uneven account of events and have factual errors and bias dependent upon the dating and authorship, and must be quoted with qualification and interpreted taking many other historical factors into account.

Verse 19

O Englonde, great cause thou haste glad for to be,
Compared to the londe of promys syon,
Thou atteynest my grace to stande in that degre
Through this gloryous Ladyes supportacyon,
To be called in every realme and regyon
The holy lande, Oure Ladyes dowre;
Thus arte thou named of olde antyquyte.

O England, thou hast great cause to be glad
Compared to the land of promised Zion
Thou attainest my grace to stand in that degree
Through this glorious Lady's support
To be called in every realm and region
The Holy Land, Our Lady's dowry;
Thus art thou named of old antiquity.

Verses 20 and 21

And this is the cause, as it apereth by lyklynesse,
In the is belded newe Nazareth, a mancyon
To the honoure of the hevenly empresse
And of hir moste gloryous salutacyon,
Chyef pryncypyll and grounde of oure salvacyon,
Whan Gabryell sayd at olde Nazereth 'Ave',
This joy here dayly remembred for to be.

And this is the cause, as appears to be most likely,
In thee is built new Nazareth, a mansion
To the honour of the heavenly empress

And of Her most glorious salutation
Chief principle and ground of our salvation
When Gabriel said at old Nazareth, 'Hail',
This joy is to be remembered here daily.

O gracyous Lady, glory of Jerusalem,
Cypresse of Syon and Joye of Israel,
Rose of Jeryco and Sterre of Bethleem,
O gloryous Lady, our askynge nat repell,
In mercy all wymen ever thou doste excell, Therfore, blissed Lady, graunt thou thy great grace
To all that the devoutly visyte in this place.

O gracious Lady, glory of Jerusalem,
Cypress of Zion and Joy of Israel,
Rose of Jericho and Star of Bethlehem,
O glorious Lady, do not reject our requests
Thou dost excel all women in mercy
Therefore, blessed Lady, grant Thou Thy great grace
To all that devoutly visit this place.

The Shrine, then, clearly after 1066, was a manorial land-holding held from the crown and until the dissolution remained so, under the guardianship of the Augustinian Canons. This estate of the Walsingham Shrine was conveyed and assigned to the Canons by the powers granted to the High Sheriffs, Hugh de Clare and Roger Bigot, acting in the name of the King. However, for the Shrine's first 120 years since its foundation, it was attended on and promoted by local people. They, like the water carriers at Cana (John 2:9), were privy to and highly involved in the foundational events of the building and the foundational setting of the Holy House of Nazareth. This Royal Shrine, then, has obscure documentary evidence, but before 1066 was probably known in royal circles through King

Edward's court and family. These beginnings and this obscurity is referred to by the author of the printed version of the Pynson Ballad in the final verse. This enquiry into the identity of the person known as Richeldis is a response in part to the royal command that our enquiry should provide a clearer understanding of this matter.

The Pynson Ballad makes the date of foundation absolutely clear as being in the reign of King Edward: 1061. King Henry VII, who made a pilgrimage before his famous victory in the Battle of Stoke to Walsingham, was beholden to Our Lady's protection and intercession in a personal manner. His victory at Stoke, which resolved for all time the divisive antagonism of the Houses of York and Lancaster, was of great importance to Henry and the realm. Following his great and historic victory, he bestowed upon the Chapel the Royal Standard in honour of Mary the Mother of God. This gift is a reminder not only of Henry VII's devotion to the Shrine of Walsingham, but refers to his victory as a resolution of civil strife at last resolved, as the great gift of his reign over England ,bestowed through the intercession of Our Blessed Lady of the Salutation and Annunciation. England (her dowry) should ever be a place of peace where the King reigns as part the kingdom of Christendom, of which Jesus Christ is the everlasting King. There is within the Pynson Ballad a clear acceptance of the Shrine's date of foundation and its royal ownership from the time of 1066. The attribution of the date as 'during the reign of King Edward', using the formula cited in the Domesday Book, underpins the description of Walsingham as a land-holding belonging to King William.

Notes

1 Henry VIII, in contradiction to his policy of dissolution, demanded that the artistic and intellectual heritage of these great abbeys and monasteries should be preserved as of both historical and intellectual importance. He recognised that the ecclesiastic historical and intellectual and artistic legacy of a thousand years of endeavour were of great importance in the life and future of his kingdom.

2 This Papal acknowledgement of Henry's defence of the Catholic Faith remains a valued acknowledgement of Henry's loyalty to the Patriarch of the West, the Roman Pontiff at this time. It is also an acknowledgement of Henry's learned defence of the Sacramental Church over and against the doctrines of Luther and the other European reformists. However, King Henry decided that the national Church of England should be ordered to the Crown and through the implementation of these precepts aligned the ancient Catholic Church of England and the British Isles with the Protestant reformed churches of Europe, over and against the Catholic Church of the apostles and early fathers.

3 The ballad records that 'the Lady was a noble widowe, sometime Lady of this town'; this ballad written after the foundation of the Shrine clearly is a confused account of the Lady's status. We know that the Lady of the town was, in 1061, Edith the 'rich and fair', married to Harold. It records that she was no longer 'Lady of this Towne', which implies that this part of the ballad was written sometime after the Shrine's Foundation and the battle of Hastings 1066, and has conflated the events in regard to the Lady of the Manor. The use of the word 'town', as a description of Walsingham Manor, shows that the writer was not a first-hand witness of these events but recorded them sometime after 1066.

4 J. Leland, *Joannis Lelandi Antiquarii De Rebus Collectanea*, T. Hearne (ed.) (London, 1715).

5 *Domesday Book*, P. Brown (ed.), general editor J. Morris (Chichester: Phillimore, 1984).

6 *Domesday Book, Norfolk*, S. Morris (ed.) (Chichester: Phillimore, 1984), p. 1, item 40. Harold held Walsingham before 1066.

7 'Tweyne' may mean 'two' or 'twin' here. See also verses 8 and 9.

8 This could also read as 'in what manner placed'.

9 The title *matrone* describes a married woman of dignity and honour who is in charge of a complex domestic process or operation.

10 'Goostly' means 'devout' (rather than 'ghostly').

4

The Augustinians' Priory Charter

There has been among many English writers, historians and editors of the past two hundred years some misunderstanding of the rules and duties of this very ancient order of religious men and women in the Catholic Church since Apostolic times. For four hundred years, since the time of the dissolution of the monasteries in England, there has been a failure to understand and appreciate the social impact of the monastic orders. Most of these negative assessments have been copied and translated from the tainted and scurrilous indictments used as 'evidence' in the suppression and sequestration of these so-called monasteries.

Erasmus, following his first visit to the Walsingham Shrine and subsequent to his second visit as a lay member of the Canons Regular, poured scorn upon these so-called proceedings and pointed out the great wonder that nowhere in the land of many thousands of religious houses was there to found one single worthy monk, canon, priest or abbot. These show trials found all guilty and purloined their estates, wealth and any valuables in their possession which were arbitrarily seized and sold (unless, of course, the accused admitted guilt and became crown witnesses for the prosecution). This is the pattern through the ages of all tyrannical governments; that so many historians and writers should, without due diligence, accept these tracts of 'evidence' at face value is a cause of regret.

Many historians in eminent places of learning, founded upon the medieval religious halls of study (and, for example, the editors of Dugdale's *Monasticon* and others) erroneously believe that the Canons Regular were introduced into England after the year 1100 or after the Norman Conquest, may have been unaware of the fact that it was only after the eleventh century that the Canons Regular were so styled. Nevertheless, upon the irrefutable records of the Catholic Church, these same orders of ecclesiastics were commonly titled religious or regular clerics and were founded in the first century. It is also true that there was a reorganisation and periodic revival of this widespread order, centred in France, Italy and the Low Countries at this particular time and that some of these newly-constituted congregations followed the Conqueror and the 'Fighting' Bishops to these lands together with their Norman appointees such as Lanfranc, Archbishop of Canterbury. However the Canons Regular is the oldest order of Christendom and was an essential component of the minster in England from the time of the earliest foundations in the fifth century. Following the death of Henry II up to the death of Edward II, 54 new houses were founded where the Canons Regular were not already established. Until the time of the Great Plague the Canons Regular flourished. However, in the service of the dying and the sick, and due to the fact that they lived very closely to their urban congregations, the Black Death decimated these Canons Regular to such an extent that on 19th March 1519, Cardinal Wolsey, in his capacity as

Papal Legate, issued the Roman *Statuta* which were to be observed by all Austin Canons. These Papal statutes provide for the union of all Austin Canons. Yet, despite this consolidation, Abbot Gasquet computes that 91 houses of regular canons were suppressed and abolished by the dissolution's inquisition irregular courts. It is of passing interest in the understanding of the wide interlocking land-holdings of Earl Harold and Edith that Thurgaston in Norfolk was a gift land bequest of Edith the Fair to the Eastholm monastery, and that it was the place where Walter Hilton wrote the *Scala perfectionis* in 1400.

St Frideswide's, founded for Canons Regular at Castle Tower by Robert d'Oiley and translated to Osney in 1149, so Cardinal Newman writes, 'became a nursery for secular students subject to the Chancellor's jurisdiction'. The streams of history often reveal eddies and echoes of the past. For instance, some thirty-four years ago (at the time of writing) in 1980, the Congregation of the Canons Regular returned to Bodmin in Cornwall, where they had in the tenth century a beautiful priory in honour of Saint Mary and Saint Petroc.

At the beginning of the reign of Henry I, the person Geoffrey, custodian at that time of the Walsingham Shrine of the Salutation and Annunciation, had made preparation to join the second crusade. The Shrine had been founded and established for over a hundred years. It was, and remained until the dissolution, a royal land-holding and so it remains. The person named as Geoffrey in the LDB of Norfolk of 1088, whose status as a third-ranking holder and whose holdings were not extensive, did not include Walsingham Manor at that time. His holdings in 1088 were held directly from

Count Alan, Duke of Brittany, William's son-in-law and Roger Bigot High Sheriff and Earl of Norfolk, who were acting directly for the King together with Roger de Clare as signatories to the Charter. Geoffrey was therefore most probably either an illegitimate son of Count Alan, Roger Bigot or the King himself. The other possibility is that he was low-born but had, through personal valour in the service of the King William's army, achieved great deeds and been rewarded with lands and wealth. The weight of the scarce evidence available favours illegitimacy and service, for which he was rewarded. First-generation illegitimacy under Norman rule was regarded as a potential threat to succession and therefore, apart from land-holding, no titles would be granted. Through subsequent generations the prefix Fitz could be adopted; we note that one John Fitz Geoffrey, son of Geoffrey Fitz Peter, died in 1213 (DNB), Fitz Peter Earl of Essex and Justiciar of England.

The Domesday record regarding Geoffrey places his holdings in 1088 into three important categories. In the first entry of this list, which begins with King William's own holdings and follows in an order of precedence; the land-holdings of Count Alan of Brittany, the King's son-in-law, rank third. This is significant as the Count's major holdings were in the north, especially Yorkshire. Under Count Alan, Geoffrey held Bringham in the Hundred of Holt. This is a strategic holding commanding the Western routes from the Eastern ports of the Danelaw into the hinterland areas of the Wash. These were strategically important in late Norman times for the defence of Peterborough and the Mercian Great River Ouse. Of his ten land-holdings, the following had been held by Earl Harold before 1066 and were therefore held directly from William:

Islington in the Hundred of Freebridge: a Manorial Holding
Hillington in the Hundred of Freebridge
Bringham in the Hundred of Freebridge
Wheatacre in the Clavering Hundred
Terrington in the Hundred of Freebridge
Chedgrave in the Loddon Hundred.

Five of the ten land-holdings were formerly held by Harold or his men. This underlines the importance of Geoffrey and his close association with senior Norman magnates, especially Count Alan, who abducted Edith the Fair's daughter from the royal Wilton Convent to marry, and protect the land-holdings which belonged to Edith before 1066.

Geoffrey held Attlebridge with Bishop William and his other holdings with Eudo son of Spirwic and in the Deepwade Hundred with Ralph Baynard. Sometime after 1088, Walsingham must have come into his tenure as custodian of the Shrine. However, his holdings are remarkable for the number of churches recorded as in his possession:

In Attlebridge One Church with 6 acres 6 pence
In Wheatacre Two Churches with 60 acres in alms
In Chedgrave One church 50 acres and meadow one acre, value two *orae*.

These are clearly in Geoffrey's tenure and the Attlebridge properties of the church are described in the Austin Canons' charters as part of their custodial holdings.

If we are in fact correct in the surmise that Geoffrey in the LDB is the father or grandfather of 'Geoffrey' described in 1169, so much incidental evidence can be judged as giving a possible identity to the person named in the Austin Canon's cartulary record.

According to the charter, instructions were given to Edwy his 'clerk' (probably his 'priest at the Shrine') to dispose of the Shrine and appurtenances as follows. The charter details all the appurtenances that belonged to the Shrine, together with the Church of All Saints and Saint Peter's, which belonged to Great and Little Walsingham as privately endowed foundations, which were held before 1066 by Ketel and Ulfketel, who were probably Edith the Fair's half-brothers as shown in the will of their mother Wulfhilda (see Appendix B). The land-holdings detailed in the 1088 LDB are intact and remain with the Shrine appurtenances with no additional gifts reported, excepting the Church of All Saints. This gift of custodianship obviously comprises of some wealth although the value is not shown in 1088, being assessed as Harold's lands in Fakenham and now belonging to William. The Austin Canons, however, are given custody of the All Saints Church, for which they would, under the Bishop's direction, have to provide a priest and all other services for the church in Great Walsingham.

It was common practice that any knight going to join the Crusades would sell or mortgage property to fund what was a very expensive and lengthy campaign in the service of Jesus Christ's Catholic Church. The first and second crusades were predominantly organised and planned under the leadership of Louis, King of the Franks. Therefore, it is highly unlikely that these matters were left until the day of departure. The charter refers to the passing of the custody of the Shrine from that day of departure to his priest cleric in Walsingham and the legalities of the transaction require the signatures of the High Sheriffs or Earls of East Anglia, Roger Bigot and Roger de Clare, who alone in this matter could act on behalf of the monarch, at this time King Stephen. This once more emphasises the royal ownership of the Walsingham Shrine of Our Blessed Lady of the Annunciation. The Shrine then, following the upheavals of the Norman and Angevin dynasties, was not the wealthy international place of pilgrimage that it later became. We recall that private ownership of places of worship was widespread under Anglo-Saxon patronage, and was perceived under both Rome and Norman rule as a matter to be regularised and established under church episcopal jurisdiction. This was not achieved in the case of Walsingham until at least 1153 under Bishop Turbus following the translation of the Cathedral from Elmenham to Norwich.

Thus the Canons Regular of the Augustinian congregation were chosen to act as custodians of the Shrine of Walsingham. They were a regular order, always subject (except in exceptional circumstances) to the local episcopate; they were then distinguished markedly from abbatial rule and vows of obedience of orders such as the Benedictines and Cistercians. The charter requires that the Austin Canons build a Priory in which the Shrine would be enclosed, in continuance of their work to administer to the people of Great and Little Walsingham, together with a college for educating poor scholars and sustaining them at an appropriate hall of residence. This local place of pilgrimage, which had survived a century of upheaval, uprisings and many changes of dynastic rule, was still a modest foundation, the founder herself having fled the country with her daughter, probably before 1076. The care and maintenance of this holy place near the Chapel of Saint Laurence in the Manor of Walsingham was in the joint royal jurisdiction of Roger Bigot and the Earl de Clare,

High Sheriffs acting for the King. The local remaining freemen and the artisans of the Manor, who were witnesses to the miraculous events of the year 1061, would certainly have taken care of the Shrine and made known the great graces they witnessed. The work of Our Blessed Lady became more widely known and the Holy House of Nazareth revered as her place of healing, making manifest the Good News of Her Son Jesus the Christ. This holy place was ever a humble refuge for the great and poor alike; it flourished modestly and grew in honour, not through noble patronage or the words of the learned, but through the humble efforts of the poor and afflicted, the halt and the lame. Alongside it from its beginning was the Chapel of Saint Laurence, the consecrated place of worship endowed by Edith the Fair and her loving husband Earl Harold, later King of England. They had built a chapel dedicated to the same saint and martyr at Waltham Abbey in Essex and this devotion to Saint Laurence is illuminating of our understanding of Medieval Anglo-Saxon religious piety and devotion.

Laurence, deacon and martyr, was the senior administrator of the congregation of Rome's treasury of funds set aside to help the poor and homeless. It was a position which the proto-martyr, Saint Steven, had held in Jerusalem (Acts 6:1–6). In 257, the Emperor Valerian began a policy aimed at reducing the influence of the Christian Church through the systematic persecution of its members among the wealthy and influential upper classes. All church property was confiscated and public and private meetings were forbidden. Pope Sixtus II and his Roman clergy were executed on 7th August 258 and Saint Laurence on 10th. This much is taken from contemporary records of the

Church. The martyr and saint were honoured widely in the early Romano English church.

Constantine the Great, proclaimed Emperor on English soil, gained power through the dynamic bravery of his British Legions. He is reputed to have built the first oratory dedicated to the saint, which was one of the stations on the itinerary of the graves of the Roman martyrs.

Laurence was given three days by the Emperor to gather up all the Church's treasure and deliver it to the Senate, in order to save himself from execution. Instead, he took the time to make the entire treasure safe through disbursement to places of safety, including the chalice used at the Last Supper. For this act of defiance, he was executed on 10th August: three days after the others had been slaughtered. His successful efforts to save the Holy Chalice of Grail gave rise to the Arthurian legends and because of the early involvement of the English Holy Roman Emperor Constantine; he was a very popular early saint and martyr named in the Anglo-Saxon martyrologies. Constantine was a much revered emperor and his close association with this early Christian martyr made Saint Laurence renowned amongst the old English nobility, who prized their close association with the early Roman Church. Saint Laurence, then, is part of the foundation of the Holy Shrine of Walsingham and has an honoured place in the English calendar. His association with Edith the Fair and Harold at Waltham and Walsingham gives verisimilitude to our search for understanding of the truth of the Shrine's foundation and remarkable survival.

The Priory Charter records the Church of All Saints as part of the bequest drawn up by Edwy and assigned by the High Sheriff's Bigot and de Clare to the Austin Canons. This most probably refers to the old Chapel, which may have been reordered during the intervening hundred years and given the associative dedication of Mary Mother of all Saints as a public place of worship. The start of the reign of Henry II as the possible trigger for custodianship to pass to the Austin Canons is problematic; he was a Norman ruler of England and clashed with his Archbishop, Thomas a Becket, and demanded his murder in circumstances which outraged Christian Europe. However, he was, as part of the extensive reparations required and compelled to revive and repair the Church and Monastery of Waltham Abbey, where Harold was buried, according to legend, and the abiding memories of the Waltham Abbey communities.

This foundation under Cnut with which Harold and his wife Edith were so closely involved is somewhat ironic. The choice of Waltham Abbey may be pure coincidence, but nonetheless is a very appropriate admonishment for the actions of his Norman ancestors, which at the time of the Conquest were subject to Papal disapproval and sanctions which the Conqueror largely ignored. From this time of the custodianship passing from private hands into the guardianship of the Austin Canons, the popularity and subsequent fame and wealth of Walsingham began to prosper and grow, mainly because of royal patronage. It began quietly in the reign of Edward the Confessor, and, for four centuries following, was one of the most widely-venerated shrines in the whole of Europe.

5

The Normans to the House of Windsor

FROM 1066 TO 1087, King William was, with great energy and determination, embroiled in a series of local and regional uprisings throughout England. He was preoccupied with affairs of state in Normandy and England, which had political and dynastic implications for the Scandinavian empire.

The Walsingham Shrine had been founded in 1061, only five years before the Conquest, probably by the wife of William's enemy, King Harold. He obviously did not suppress the Shrine or have it sequestrated by the Norman Bishops. He clearly left the Shrine to continue as a local place of pilgrimage. This was undoubtedly because it had been founded in the reign of Edward the Confessor, and because of Edward's connection with Edith as lady of the Manor. William was adamant that he was the rightful heir of King Edward, and therefore he was at great pains to maintain and promote that connection by which he claimed the rightness of his actions and the support of the Papacy and the ecclesiastical community in England. In this manner, he could rightly condemn Harold's claim to the throne and bolster his own. However, Edith, as the wife of Harold and mother of his children, the Visionary and builder of the Shrine, would have been expunged from the record. The Shrine of Our Blessed Lady was always referred to and described as having been founded in the reign of Edward the Confessor. It follows that no references were allowed to become part of the historical record that in any way referred to the Visionary founder, except in the vaguest term of Rychold. Edward had spent the greatest part of his youth in Normandy, where he had been exiled. Born at Islip, near Oxford, he was revered by his many Norman friends as a saintly and trustworthy friend, brother-in-arms and later King. Therefore, for two overriding reasons, the Shrine's Visionary, Edith the Fair, was removed from the record.

The first reason was the Norman and European opposition to what was regarded as the cult of Anglo-Saxon royal saints, which was, as discussed above, opposed by the Norman Archbishop, Lanfranc of Canterbury. Secondly, it was clearly a matter of concern to the Conqueror that there would be no opposition centred on Harold's family, especially his sons who had opposed the Normans in the West from their base in Dublin. Therefore, both Harold and his wife Edith were obliterated from English history following the Battle of Hastings and their loving union as man and wife described as illegitimate, although several recent English kings such as Canute were married in the same *mores danico* manner. Thus, the Shrine would always be designated as founded in the reign of Edward and the visionary known as the Highly Favoured Lady (which, of course, is the well-known title of Our Lady of the Salutation as well as the name of Edith, wife of Harold). However, the Shrine was left as it was before the Conquest as a foundation of the reign of Edward the Confessor. The Holy House had been built and erected by the local artisans and this close involvement and detailed knowledge of the visions helped to ensure that the Chapel was always maintained and cherished and that local loyalty was paramount in maintaining and promoting the Shrine through thanksgiving for favours and prayers granted, the sick healed and the afflicted comforted and calmed. It is probable that King Edward would have been aware and supportive of this sign of Our Lady's favour at Walsingham and that this possible Royal approval, now destroyed, was a further major reason for the Shrine to remain in Royal hands with a direct connection to King Edward, with Harold denied the title of King.

The land of the Manor of Walsingham, as the Domesday Book reveals, was a royal holding and although situated in a remote rural area this royal protection was exercised through the appointed custodian landholder. Although a religious man, William kept all senior Church appointments subject to his sanction and although strongly opposed by Rome, his successors, as far as circumstances would allow, maintained this policy. Thus, the Norman ruling dynasty until 1154, when Henry II succeeded to the throne, ensured that Walsingham remained a local shrine from the time of Edward. The Royal Shrine's custodian landholder held the Chapel and its manorial lands in private, but could not dispose of it without the direct consent of the English monarch. This benign and subdued interest was reviewed when, in the reign of Stephen, the person known as Geoffrey mortgaged or leased his possessions and left these shores to join the second crusade. Royal ownership was retained and custody was granted to the Austin Canons, following jurisdiction passing to the Bishop of Norwich.

From the time of Henry II, the Angevin dynasty ruled England from Aquitaine and accumulated more territories in France. They did not regard England as their primary home until King John lost most of their French possessions. Following from the disastrous reign of King John (in terms of French dynastic sovereignty over the British Isles whereby he lost many French territories), he and the succeeding Plantagenets from the time of Henry III, who reigned from 1207 to 1272, concentrated their armed forces and diplomacy on expanding their territories in the British Isles and becoming a powerful independent state, including some minor French possessions. Until Henry III, English kings had resided in (and for extended periods had ruled from) France.

The Royal Shrine at Walsingham, enclosed in the Priory of the Austin Canons at this time, was and remained a local place of pilgrimage without the prestige of royal patronage from the Angevin Royal house, who regarded England as a major department of the Norman Empire.

This changed dramatically with the coronation of Henry III, at the age of nine. On gaining his majority, the focus of his reign became the consolidation of his English possessions and he with his advisors sought to re-establish an English identity from the time prior to Edward the Confessor. In 1226, Henry III, at the age of 19, visited the Shrine and this royal visit was followed by many others. From this time it became a celebrated place of pilgrimage throughout Europe. It was from here on to become the Royal Shrine of England, with a provenance that went back to the time of King Edward and thus became part of English national identity as the Dowry of Mary the Mother of God. This, among many other diplomatic and armed victories achieved by Henry III and his son, Edward, established England as a kingdom with dominium over the British Isles; Edward and his successors, often through force of arms, consolidated their suzerainty throughout the British Isles. However, as a distinct and separate sovereign state, yet an integrated part of Christian Europe, this nation was also claiming rightly that it was a Christian nation whose beginnings dated to the time of Alban and the other proto-martyrs, Julius and Aaron. The ancient title of Mary's Dowry was an essential component of the identity of the British Romano Church and thus important to Henry and his successors in establishing England as an ancient nation in the European community of Christendom. The Walsingham Shrine of Our Lady of the Salutation and Annunciation, with its ancient replica of The Holy House of Nazareth, confirmed these historical facts and was no doubt a factor that caused Henry VIII to delay its destruction and dissolution when, with failing health, he possibly allowed the zealots to dissolve what he knew should be saved. Henry III made at least another three pilgrimages, in 1241, 1280 and 1296. His son, Edward I, made many visits to the Shrine during his long reign, including a three-day vigil in 1315.

Foreign princes and kings were given safe passage and the King's protection on innumerable occasions and King Edward III, in 1361, granted nine pounds toward the expenses of John, Duke of Brittany for this pilgrimage, together with the King's licence to reside for this purpose away from London. To his nephew, the Duke of Anjou, who was one of his French hostages, the King also granted safe passage and his protection. It was the same King who gave safe conduct for King David of Scotland and twenty knights to make this most holy pilgrimage. The Shrine prospered and with it the Priory of the Austin Canons. However, they held all wealth in common and there were strict regulations with regard to their duties in administering the sacraments, singing the daily office, giving alms to the poor and needy and educating the young. They were required by statute to send young men of the required ability to the appropriate halls of residence at university, probably Ely, Norwich and Cambridge, and pay all necessary expenses. The canons were also responsible for the maintenance, refurbishment and care of the Priory, the Holy Chapel and all its accoutrements, a specified number of beds and food for pilgrims and the welfare of all who sought help in distress. They were accountable to the local bishop for the provision of a priest to all churches in their care and two inspections each year were carried out by the congregations' legates. All property and other valuables had to be identified and an inventory kept for the King's pleasure as a royal holding. Many historians today seem to be ignorant of these statutes and presume that this wealth was available to the canons. It is obvious to all that in catering and providing for the many pilgrims, poor and wealthy alike, that many enterprising townspeople would prosper. The whole area of Norfolk, from Fakenham to Wells and beyond, such as those along the Palmer's Way from London through New Market and Thetford, and from the north through King's Lynn, prospered. All, however, knew and rejoiced that it was through the grace of Our Lady's prayers and her relief and care for all in need; that was treasured here above all else.

The Canons Regular as custodians were also granted land tithes and rents; however, in 1255, Henry III confirmed the substantial benefactions of eight wealthy donors. Whilst in 1281 Edward I, while at Walsingham, confirmed to the Priory Canons the churches of Saint Peter of Great Walsingham, Saint Clement and Saint Andrew of Burnham, Saint Andrew Bedington and the communities of Tymelthorpe and Owelton. This and other benefactions provided an annual income of nearly £80 but, as can be seen above, with this income came responsibility for upkeep, repair and refurbishment. Through time, this is likely to have sometimes become a burden and a drain upon their dwindling income.

The income of the Walsingham Shrine of £80 pounds per annum to the custodians should be compared with Harold's income in 1066 of approximately £3,000 per annum, to give us some idea of the scale and influence of the Austin Canons as minimal compared to the wealth of the ruling elite. It is a matter of fact that the Priory of Walsingham was established and maintained in perpetuity to serve and protect the Shrine of Our Blessed Lady. The Austin Canons, referred to as Canons Regular, were commissioned to act only with the permission and authority of the local bishop: the Bishop of Norwich. The canons were not monks belonging to a religious order, such as the Benedictines, with abbatial rule and a set of regulations ordered on monastic life; they were canons of the Cathedral within their own congregation and priory. They attended daily services in the priory church but served the local community or parish churches given into their charge. They were required to provide education to all who would prosper with it and to serve the sick and protect the poor. Therefore, they were subject to regular visits and inspections from their own order, but also, if required, by any episcopal commissions convened by the Bishop. They elected their own prelates, such as a prior, a sub-prior, a cellarer and a librarian. They lived together as a community and were required to act and dress soberly, paying attention to cleanliness without show or ostentation. Clement V sanctioned the appropriation of the church of Saint Peter, Great Walsingham, at the value of £10 of their patronage, the church to be served by one of the canons.

As is shown above, Great Walsingham was a holding separate from the Manor of Walsingham and finally confirmed in patronage only as part of the custody holding of the Austin Canons from 1314. These examples are given to provide the enquirer with a little understanding of the life and wealth of the Priory and the Shrine of Walsingham, which is little known and which has been so sadly distorted by the fabricated evidence gathered by 'the dissolution commissioners' whose only purpose was to malign and denigrate the custodians in order to justify the confiscation of all valuables given to the Shrine custodians during four hundred years of devotion, despite the fact that it was a crown land-holding and sold by the crown; following the dissolution, the proceedings taken against the Austin Friars made no acknowledgement of this fact.

The following examples are set down to correct this distortion of the evidence. In May 1385, the Prior and canons of Walsingham paid the King in tribute a fine of £100 to secure the alienation to them in mortmain of considerable lands and manors in Norfolk, including the manors of Great and Little Ryburgh of the value of £40 per annum, to find four chaplains, canons or regular, to celebrate daily in the newly built chapel of Saint Anne within the said Priory for the good estate of Joan, widow of Thomas de Felton, knight, and for her soul after death and for the soul of the said Thomas, Thomas his son and others, and to find a light daily therein at High Mass. In 1465, Prior Thomas and his convent obtained a licence in mortmain for the acquisition of lands, tenements and rents, in relief of their poor possessions to the value of £40 that they might pray for the good estate of the King and Queen and for their souls after death.

Through the fourteenth and fifteenth centuries, there are recorded many visitations that dealt with some matters of corruption and lack of discipline; these records, however, do not reveal evidence of consistent indiscipline and all were dealt with to ensure the restoration of good order among the canons. In March 1384, the custody of the Priory was given by the King to the sub-prior acting on behalf of his kinsman, Roger, son and heir of the late Earl of March, a minor, in consequence of contention between the sub-prior and John Snoryng, prior, the latter being wasteful of its revenue in his desire to procure the position of abbot. This action was taken on advice from a commission, presided over by Michael de la Pole, the chancellor appointed to inquire into the dispute.

In this dispute, we see the King, on the advice of the Earl of March, Roger Bigot, a minor, as an active participant in matters concerning the Shrine of the Salutation at Walsingham. As we follow the evidence, the royal ownership and their active involvement underlines the veracity of the Domesday Book recording, firstly, the Visionary of Walsingham as Edith the wife of King Harold, who is recorded as owner of the Manor before 1066. From the time of King William, it remained a royal holding and although protected was bereft of royal patronage until the time of the reign of Henry III. It is quite clear from the evidence so far that the Shrine of Our Lady of Walsingham was the work of Edith the Fair, 'Richeldis', and yet we have very little understanding of the pious Lady referred to in many recent publications as 'the concubine' of King Harold II. However, the record of the Cambridge Domesday book and its clear references to 'Edith the Fair' taken from the Latin text *Edeva Puella* provide first-hand records of a very remarkable and powerful English noblewoman who played a prominent role in the governance of the realm from 1020 until possibly 1076.

6

Edith the Fair and Rich

THE WALSINGHAM SHRINE was most probably founded in the reign of Edward the Confessor, in 1061. King Edward was the son of Aethelred II, 'the Unready', and his second wife, Emma, the daughter of Richard II of Normandy. Following Aethelred's death in 1016, the Anglo-Saxon element, with their vision of an independent Christian kingdom, took control with the support of Harold and Hardecanute, and Edward lived in exile until 1041. He returned to the court of his half-brother, Hardecanute, and became King of England in 1042.

The Anglo-Saxon/Old English armies had been defeated at Assandun by Canute and they forced Edmund to yield the kingdom. In this decisive battle, many English warrior noblemen died, and one of their great battle commanders was Ulfcytel the Brave; he was, according to the Chronicler, one of the nation's great men, who was married to Wulfhilda, daughter of Aethelred II. He was, therefore, married to King Edward's sister or half-sister. The date of this battle is 1016, where Thorkell the Tall, who had changed sides to be with Canute, his fellow Dane, was the victorious leader of the armies of Canute opposed to the Anglo-Saxon warrior class of Englishmen. Thorkell was renowned as one of the greatest Jomsviking Broderbund and was a professional Scandinavian warrior, who is reputed to have killed Ulfcytel. Under the Scandinavian honour code, he was then duty-bound to marry Ulfcytel's widow, Wulfhilda. This protected family members and safeguarded inherited land and property in acknowledgement of the bravery and honour of the warrior dying in valour on the battlefield. The vast majority of the noble warrior ruling class at this time were fortunate to survive into their forties and many of their noblewomen were married two or three times, out of necessity to maintain their homes and families. Being widowed with young families, together with extensive property and family wealth supported by grandmothers and dowager beneficiaries, the women were in some cases powerful and wealthy, in fact a stable and leading part of ruling dynasties.

Ulfcytel was a leading East Anglian councillor, known as Snillingri in the Scandinavian sagas, which can mean 'the Bold and the Brave'. His major landholdings were in Cambridgeshire and it is within this family of Ulfcytel and Wulfhilda that we have reference to Edeva or Edith the Fair, recorded in Domesday of Cambridge, taken from the Latin record *Edeva Puella.* However, it is relevant to our search for the identity of the Lady of the Manor of Walsingham to understand some important appointments made by Edward the Confessor in the first three years of his rule. He was crowned in 1042 and appointed the Great Earls: Siward, Macbeth's enemy in Northumbria; Leofric in Mercia; and Godwin in Wessex. These appointments confirmed the status quo in Mercia, Northumbria and Wessex; however, the most troublesome and vulnerable of the earldoms had been East Anglia of the

Danelaw. King Edward was a careful king and prudent ruler who recognised the need to ensure that these appointments would no longer hold these titles and lands as hereditary dynasties. He therefore made them, together with Harold, who he appointed Earl of East Anglia, dependent upon land-holdings and estates of crown lands that would form the wealth and operating base of the ealdorman as part of the office, and not held as committal lands. In recompense, he made over some part of the royal revenues in the form of 1/3 penny of revenues from places like Norwich, which formed part of these office holders' revenues but were controlled by the exchequer.

Therefore the great regional barons were tied more closely to the monarch and less able to create regional suzerainty as a form of localised or regionalised independent powerbases. Thus, for instance, the extensive land and burgess holdings of Ulfcytel in East Anglia, which passed to Thorkell the Tall from 1016 and his family (together with Wulfhilda, who we noted above he was obliged to marry), *remained* as committal holdings and were not part of the holdings granted on the appointment of the office of Earl of East Anglia. Thus, when Harold was appointed by King Edward, his holdings were entirely separate from the Ulfcytel/Thorkell lands centred on Cambridge, although undoubtedly Ulfcytel as advisor to King Aethelred was the recent Earl of East Anglia. Thus we come to appreciate the strategic importance of Edith the Fair's holdings, which could only pertain if her relationship to Thorkell the Tall was through the bloodline, through marriage or solemn adoption.

The appointments of the regional baronies at the beginning of Edward's reign coincided with the King's marriage to Edith of Rutland, Earl Godwin's daughter, and soon after of the marriage of Earl Godwin's son to Edith the Fair, together with Harold's appointment as Earl of East Anglia. This date for the marriage of Edith to Harold is confirmed by examination of the chronology of their dates of birth and the spread of dates of their known offspring. If we accept that Edith was the daughter of Ulfcytel who died in 1016 at the Battle of Assundan, then by 1042 she would have been 26 years of age, which is very late for marriage at this time. As daughter of Thorkell by Ulfcytel's widow, her inheritance would have been safeguarded, but only in the event of being Thorkell's only remaining offspring, and daughter of the daughter of King Aethelred and the great Jomsviking commander, who was King Canute's commander-in-chief and who had acted directly with the King's authority for a time over the whole realm in the absence of Canute. The marriage of such a powerful magnate's daughter would no doubt have been very problematic.

These most important major dynastic moves on behalf of King Edward reveal a wise and decisive ruler who had a clear vision of his responsibilities in exercising control over a war-ravaged kingdom. Queen Edith, Edward's wife, was the elder sister of Harold and daughter of Earl Godwin. Through her mother, Gytha Thorkelsdottir, Edith inherited vast land-holdings in Northamptonshire and Rutland. Godwin senior, the father of Queen Edith, had been the close Anglo-Saxon ally of Canute and the majority of his son's family were named after the Canute family. It was therefore a priority for the new King Edward to secure his reign with the backing of Earl Godwin, Harold's father. It is from this dynastic political alliance and other connections and appointments that King Edward ensured his 26-year reign. These strategic manoeuvrings can be illuminated in detail as we examine the Little Domesday book for Cambridge, completed in 1086.

On his appointment as Earl of East Anglia, Harold had no close ties with, understanding of, or following in, East Anglia. He was born near Bosham in Wessex and had some minor holdings in Somerset and Herefordshire, which were gifts from his father's estates. This was therefore a somewhat rash appointment on behalf of King Edward, in the light of very recent Scandinavian invasions and may point to the importance of Harold's marriage to Edith the Fair, whom we know had far greater connections in the counties of the Danelaw, especially through her father Thorkell the Tall who had held the region on behalf of King Edward. Therefore, we turn once again to the Cambridgeshire Domesday as it had been the land-holding base of her possible father, Ulfcytel the Bold and Brave, whose land and burgess holdings would have passed to Thorkell the Tall and his heirs in 1016, or reverted to the Crown and appear as lands of King Edward. The survey and records of 1086 are as follows: they did not revert to the crown and therefore would have passed to Thorkell the Tall, now married to Wulfhilda, Ulfcytel's former wife; from this union they came into the possession of Edith the Fair as recorded in the Domesday Book. The following is a selected extract survey of these holdings and is first-hand evidence of Edith the Fair's status and family.

The LAND OF THE KING, as was the custom were recorded first and the account of each manorial holding refers to the owner in the reign of King Edward, in the Domesday Book for Cambridge under 'The Land of The King' are recorded William The Conqueror's holdings in the STAPLOE hundred:

Item 1. SOHAM

This opening entry sets down the important tribute and tax revenues accruing.

> SOHAM is a Manor of The King's. It answers for 9 1/2 hides.
> Land for 14 Ploughs [1140 acres].
> 16 Villagers and 16 smallholders with 12 Ploughs [1440 acres].
> 4 slaves; 2 mills at 24 shillings; from fisheries, 3500 eels; meadow for 14 ploughs, pasture for the village livestock.
> 7 fishermen there who pay to the King's presentation of fish three times a year, according to what they can.
> In total value it pays £25 a year assayed and weighed and £13 8s 4d at face value in white pence for, corn. Malt, honey and other small customary dues. Before 1066 it paid £25 at face value and three days revenue in corn, malt and honey and everything else.
> King Edward always had this manor in Lordship.[1]

This pattern of description is followed throughout and the information regarding ownership or Lordship of the itemised holding is also recorded, ensuring that we have a first-hand legal register of ownership before and following Harold's defeat in 1066:

> Item 12 in the land of the King still within the STAPLOE hundred.
>
> In Exning King William has 13 1/2 hides. Land for 34 ploughs [4080 acres].

> In Lordship seven ploughs a further 3 possible.
> 35 Villagers and 35 smallholders with 24 ploughs.
> 7 slaves, 3 mills, 20s and 7000 eels, meadow for 4 ploughs.
> Total value £53; when Godric acquired it £12; before 1066 £56.
> EDEVA the Fair, held this manor and in this manor were 7 Freemen, Edeva's men.
> They could withdraw without her permission, but she had jurisdiction of them herself.
> Each of them found cartage in the King's service, or 8d or a pledge.[2]

Here are the recorded land-holdings of Ulfcytel and, following him, Thorkell the Tall, the victor at Assundan in 1016 where Ulfcytel died, which were held by Edith the Fair as recorded in the LDB in 1088. These are land and burgess-holdings in Cambridgeshire, held by the former earls of East Anglia, of which the most recent, Ulfcytel, was a renowned Anglo-Saxon warrior, advisor and charter signatory to King Aethelred the Unready. The possibility is clear that, on the evidence of these land-holdings, Edith the Fair inherited them either from Ulfcytel's marriage to Wulfhilda or her subsequent union with Thorkell the Tall. These extensive land-holdings summarised below, of which the item for Exning is a tiny fragment, indicate the great wealth and power which signify the authority of Cnut's and Edward's regional earls.

Edith the Fair's holdings comprise four in Buckinghamshire, *c.* 77 in Cambridgeshire, six in Essex and 17 in Suffolk. These holdings total over a hundred and made her a very rich and powerful noblewoman who inherited from very powerful magnates, and whose alliance in marriage would have been of great concern to the new King Edward and the newly appointed Harold as Earl of East Anglia. Thus, it becomes apparent that Earl Harold's marriage to Edith the Fair was a matter of great importance and was probably a marriage dictated by grave dynastic imperatives. That these lands were held before 1066 by Edith the Fair is beyond dispute, and the records of her mother's last will and testament illustrate extensive familial ties between the House of Godwin and the family of Edith the Fair.

The marriage of Ulfcytel and Wulfhilda has a circumstantial provenance, yet this evidence also remains fragmentary and in some aspects is difficult to interpret. The will of Wulfgyth clearly indicates two sons named Ulfketel and Ketel and two daughters who take precedence over Edith. Clearly, the daughters of Wulfhilda are from a separate and earlier marriage, which supports the understanding that Edith was the daughter of Wulfhilda and Thorkell the Tall following his victory and the death of Ulfketel at Assundan in 1016. This would have ensured that the land-holding and wealth of Ulfcytel would not have passed to his sons on his death in 1016. However, Thorkell the Tall was a very important figure between 1016 and 1023 when he apparently returned to Denmark. As victor at Assundan, he was the second most powerful person in England as first advisor to Canute and probably King Canute's mentor and guardian as his named Jomsviking man of valour.

There are at least two separate sources which refer to Thorkell's marriage to a daughter of King Aethelred. The supplement of the Jomsviking Saga calls his wife Wulfhilda, who was wife of Ulfketel, who fell in the battle of Assundan 1016. During his close association with King Canute, Thorkell the Tall is named in various charters as Earl of East Anglia, which supports the understanding that Edith the Fair was the daughter of Wulfhilda and Thorkell, who would have inherited through the paternal line the extensive estates referred to above, as the only surviving offspring. She would then have been born between 1016 and 1023, when Thorkell the Tall was first banished and finally settled in Denmark. This chronology would be possible in the event of Edith the Fair marrying Harold in 1042/5, by which date Thorkell was dead and Edward the King of England. Further comparison of the land-holdings committed by King Edward to the ealdorman of East Anglia and the land-holdings of Edith show in their geographical proximity a clear indication that they were designed as complementary holdings and promoted a very close strategic defensive arrangement in the event of assault from any European/Danish/Scandinavian national alliance on East Anglian Danelaw territory.

Further, there is in the detail of Edith's holdings in the Cambridge Domesday further associations that identify her as the wife of Harold and the Lady of the Manor of Walsingham. The Cambridge list of land-holders has Count Alan of Brittany as the principle tenant-in-chief after 1066, holding the lands and burgess tenements of Edith the Fair. Count Alan had possession of the lands of Edith the Fair in 1088 and, acting independently of his Norman allies, he abducted Edith the Fair's daughter Gunhild from the royal convent at Wilton, although subsequently she refused to return and in turn married Alan's brother, remaining in his northern stronghold of Richmond Castle. This marriage and the correspondence of Anselm dated 1093 are further unimpeachable sources that provide us with an ever-clearer understanding of the Visionary of Walsingham as Edith the Fair, wife of King Harold II of England.

We have seen above and discussed the possible relationship of Geoffrey named as holder of the Walsingham Shrine before his departure on the second crusade and the Shrine passing from his guardianship into the care of the Austin Friars. We also have that link clearly demonstrated again in the holdings of Edith the Fair in Cambridge, as the following entries record:

Land of Count Alan

Item 63

> In Swaffham 1 Hide and three virgates Geoffrey from the Count
> Land for four ploughs. In Lordship 1; three villagers have three ploughs
> 2 slaves, 1 mill at 4s 4d and 100 eels, meadow for one plough, pasture for their livestock
> Value 40s when acquired 20s before 1066 the same
> 6 Freemen held this land under Edith, they could not withdraw without her permission but they found 3 escorts and one cartage a year for the Sheriff.

Item 7: Burwell

> In Burwell Geoffrey holds 1 hide and 1 virgate from Count Alan land for 2 ploughs they are in Lordship with 3 villagers and 2 slaves
> Meadow for one plough and pasture for the livestock
> Value 40s; when acquired 30s; before 1066 40s
> 1 freeman held this land under Edith; he could withdraw without her permission.

Item 77

> In WESTLEY (Waterless) 2 men-at-arms hold 1 hide from the Count
> Land for 2 ploughs; they are there with 4 small-holders
> The value is and always was 20s
> 7 Freemen held this land under Edith. They found cartages in the King's service; they could not withdraw without the Lady's permission.[3]

There were very strong ties between Edith's holdings from former times and the crown. The King and his court were constantly travelling and in each earldom the daily logistical support for transport and supplies was under the control of the earl and his shire reeve whenever the King was visiting. However, just as important in this period of armies moving from area to area and battle to battle to fight were the army suppliers, who were essential suppliers of land and water transport to support the professional and mercenary warriors. Thus we can understand the importance and standing of such a land-holder as Edith in this supply of cartage to the King.

However, it is evident that Edith as a land-holder before 1066 maintained her land under the Count and it is clear that her daughter Gunhild, despite her father's defeat in 1066, would still have held some form of jurisdiction over these land-holdings on the death or absence of her mother, which were likely to have been held separately by Edith as part of her hand-fast marriage to Harold, inherited from her father's estates and separate from any marriage settlement. This situation would necessitate a hand-fast marriage in the Danish manner. This points to a paternal committal of these holdings and affirms that they were in all probability in possession of Thorkell the Tall before passing to Edith, his only surviving child from his marriage to Wulfhilda, daughter of King Aelthred the Unready.

There are further details in the Cambridge Domesday records that underline the link between Edith the Fair and the House of Godwin, as follows:

Land of Count Alan

Item 1 in the Flendish Hundred

> Count Alan holds 8 hides in Fulbourne Land for thirteen ploughs
> In Lordship 4 hides; 3 Ploughs there; a further 2 possible
> 16 villagers and 10 smallholders with 8 ploughs
> 4 slaves, 1 mill at 20s; meadow for the ploughs
> The total value is and always was £15
> Young Godwin, Edeva the Fair's man, held this manor; he could not withdraw
> In the Childeath Hundred
> In the same village [Horse heath] Alwin holds one virgate of land from Count Alan
> Land for 6 Oxen 2 Smallholders, woodland for 20 pigs
> The value is and was 20s
> Godwin, Edith's man, held this land; he could not withdraw.

Item 80 in the Radfield Hundred

> Young Godwin held this land under Edith, he could not withdraw.[4]

Here we have a clear series of references before 1066 to Edith the Fair having jurisdiction over Young Godwin. This would have to be in all probability Gyrth, who eventually succeeded Harold as Earl of

East Anglia, residing in the area under Edith's control whilst growing up and becoming familiar with the customs and peoples of the Danelaw region. However, it could refer to the younger generation, such as a nephew, which would provide a sensible chronology for these events and is therefore more probable and is further evidence of the Edith of the Cambridge Domesday as Harold's wife and the Visionary of Walsingham.

The cumulative weight of this first-hand evidence supports the understanding that Edith the Fair was the wife of Harold II and held extensive lands in her own person and exercised jurisdiction over younger male members of the House of Godwin before they came to their majority. She was indeed both rich and fair as the title Richeldis clearly illustrates. It is as well to emphasise that the land-holdings thus far referred to as in the jurisdiction of Edith the Fair are at least less than half of the territories which we know belonged to her. These lands she held separately from the manorial holdings which she shared with Harold as his handfast spouse. Edith the Fair was referred to in a letter of the Abbot of Eastholm as 'keen and wise in her understanding'.[5] The cumulative weight of evidence shows both familial and strategic geographical associations of land-holdings, together with the fragmentary documentary evidence from a variety of sources, which both chronologically and historically from prime sources show both Harold and Edith as living throughout the reign of Edward the Confessor in East Anglia and at the royal court when summoned, and exercising great power and authority in the region. These records reveal Edith's close association with Count Alan of Brittany following the Conquest. It is now apparent that the Count of Brittany took over all of Edith's holdings, which were probably entailed to pass to her daughter Gunhild, who was abducted from Wilton Convent as the intended wife, firstly of Count Alan the Red, then his brother, Alan the Black. They protected her in their stronghold at Richmond Castle, Yorkshire, from the blandishments of the Archbishop of Canterbury and the predatory designs of King William II, who sought to have her returned to the convent at Wilton, thereby making her maternal estates available to the crown.

Edith's Cambridgeshire holdings and those in her name in East Anglia and the burgess holding in Canterbury can be inferred as the holdings of Thorkell the Tall, her father by the former wife of Ulfcytel, Wulfhilda, daughter of King Aethelred the Unready and half-sister to King Edward. These events then explain the flight to Denmark of Edith following the conquest with her daughter Gytha and the subsequent events in Europe concerning the latter's marriage and the resting-place of Edith the Fair. She is likely to have fled to the protection of her father Thorkell the Tall. The events which followed King Edward's appointment of Harold as Earl of East Anglia and the latter's marriage to the heiress of Thorkell the Tall confirm that Edith the Fair and Rich (Richeldis) was an important part of the initial decisions by King Edward to secure, through family relationships, the stability of East Anglia and sound political relations with Denmark and the Scandinavian countries. It is also evident that Harold and Edith were devout Christians. However, under Norman rule and the following royal Norman dynasties until the time of the Plantagenets, there was continual reference to the marriage of Harold as illegitimate. This is a misunderstanding of the situation in northern Europe, where the hand-fast marriage remained the accepted custom for at least another century. It recognised the family bond of both parties and also safeguarded the rights of noblewomen to inherit and hold extensive land and property, including burgess-holdings and the extensive lands of Christian convents; women in dual convents for men and women were more likely to hold the most senior office and often were owners of bequeathed lands, property and other valuables. It is a mistake in terms of historical understanding to refer to a hand-fast marriage as an illegitimate union and although there is no direct evidence of either a Christian canonical marriage or a hand-fast union, it remains merely an observation without any profound indication of loose adherence to the teaching of the Church, which had been clarified in very recent times with regard to the sacrament of marriage and consequently the requirement to uphold a celibate clergy.

Notes

1 *Domesday Book*, P. Brown (ed.), general editor J. Morris (Chichester: Phillimore, 1984), p. 1, item 1, 189c.

2 *Ibid.*, pp.1–2, item 12,190a.

3 *Ibid.*, p. 14, item 77, 195d.

4 *Ibid.*, p. 14, item 80, 195d.

5 F. M. Stenton, 'St. Benet's Holme and the Norman Conquest', in G. Clark (ed.), *English Historical Review*, vol. XXXVII (London: Longmans, 1922).

7

SAINT WULFSTAN OF WORCESTER

THE FOLLOWING SUMMARY of the important associations between Harold, his wife Edith and their daughter Gunhild provide support of the understanding that Edith the Fair of the Domesday record was the wife of Harold. Their daughter Gunhild, who was married to Count Alan of Brittany and the Lord of Richmond Castle, Yorkshire, are clearly associated not only with the Cambridge record but also with the Little Domesday record of Walsingham, and the Chronicle of Worcester, which provides a concise account of Harold's close friendship with Bishop Wulfstan. The lands of Harold held by Geoffrey in the Norfolk Domesday were held under the jurisdiction of Count Alan. The very strong connection between Harold, his wife Edith and the counts of Brittany is confirmed throughout the Domesday record. However, there is the evidence in the Worcester Chronicle, which underlines the piety and strong religious convictions of Harold, that add verisimilitude to the devotion of his wife Edith and their Christian marriage, despite the hostile late historical record that they were married *mores danico*.

Wulfstan completed his schooling in 1023; he began his ecclesiastical training in the time of Bishop Brith-theath, training first as a clerk at Worcester Cathedral and then being called to the priesthood in recognition of his piety and demeanour against his will. The Benedictine house at Worcester was closely associated with the Godwin family. In 1055, in the absence of Bishop Ealdred, Wulfstan was chosen to act as Prior of Worcester.

Harold was attracted to Wulfstan as a young person, and he would travel many miles to receive the latter's spiritual guidance; he remained the spiritual advisor and guide to Harold's family until his death. Bishop Ealdred was appointed Archbishop of York and thus had to resign from the seat at Worcester. On 29 August 1062, Wulfstan's election was canonically confirmed by King Edward, who invested Wulfstan with the bishopric. Under normal circumstances he would have been consecrated by his own metropolitan archbishop, Stigand; however, there were doubts about Stigand's position and he was consecrated by Archbishop Ealdred of York. The same archbishop consecrated Harold as King four years later. As bishop, Wulfstan continued to observe the monastic rule, as had his predecessor's centuries before at Canterbury. He responded to all petitioners in the manner of the great Saint Ambrose of Milan. No matter how long and arduous his journey, he would stop and pray at all chapels and churches en route. He regularly attended the shire courts and the quarterly itinerant Royal courts. Wulfstan was concerned that Christian life was not being observed as it should be and that the Danes had brought with them a permissive way of life, which should be opposed. This clash of Anglo-Saxon ancient

Christianity with the pagan ancestral worship of the Scandinavian nations was one of opposing cultures, which was a cause of so much upheaval for the whole of the tenth century.

With Harold's accession to the throne, Bishop Wulfstan became spiritual advisor and director to the King of England. He was a man of great integrity and was not involved with matters other than those reserved for the pastoral care of souls. He supported Harold and assisted him in encouraging a great moral revival in England, reform of the clergy and education and support for the poor. Harold accepted this advice from his mentor, and he was accompanied by Wulfstan, who was known throughout the realm for his holiness. They toured the northern territories and won over the people in support of their consecrated and anointed King. The Worcester Chronicle provides evidence that Wulfstan was summoned to London and witnessed the coronation of King William after his victory at Hastings. When he was ordered to surrender his pastoral staff of office as Bishop of Worcester, he responded by declaring that he would only surrender it to the king whose hand had consecrated him and placed it upright at the tomb of Edward the Confessor. William relented in the face of such holiness and calm devotion to his office, and confirmed Wulfstan as bishop. King John, *c.* 1208 used this confrontation as confirming that the King alone could rightly appoint bishops to their seats in England. King John adopted Wulfstan as his patron saint and is buried at Worcester with Wulfstan and Saint Oswald, bishop from 961-92.

In the Royal Wilton convent record of Queen Edith, wife of King Edward and sister-in-law of Edith the Fair (wife of Harold, who was brother of the Queen), there is mention of a visit by Wulfstan to Gunhild, Harold's daughter, to treat her for a persistent eye impediment. Wulfstan is reported as saying that he visited her because he owed such a great debt to her father; thus we have a chronicled visit to Harold's daughter, which supports all the chronology and brings together the Edith of the Domesday record with Queen Edith and Gunhild at the royal convent of Wilton.

The abduction, so-called, of Gunhild by Alan the Red, Count of Brittany and Norman overlord of Edith's land holdings and Gunhild's subsequent marriage to his brother Alan the Black, together with the record from the convent of Wilton of a visit from her father's great spiritual advisor Wulfstan, bishop of Worcester, indicates the important position occupied by Edith the Fair, surely rich and highly favoured, in the events immediately following the Conquest, as they affected her close family and her patrimony.

Wulfstan's widely accredited humility; his simplicity and lifelong devotion to the sick, the poor and the afflicted; and his resolute conduct in doing right in the face of kings and princes were facts acknowledged and attested by all during his lifetime. He was the exemplar of the Anglo-Saxon model of sanctity in the teeth of Scandinavian pagan worship and Norman disciplined rigour. In due course, on 21st April 1203, he was raised to the altars and canonised. Above all, he is remembered and revered by his compatriots for his God-given ability to heal the sick and afflicted and perform miracles of holiness. Harold and Edith the Fair and Rich obviously had a very happy and blessed marriage, despite the hostile remarks of the Conqueror and his followers. The Anglo-Saxon Christian Church throughout the tenth century had resisted the pagan religions of the Northmen. Their final triumph was the conversion of Canute and the subsequent reign of Saint Edward the Confessor, which of course includes the marvel of the visions of Walsingham witnessed by Edith the Fair and Rich, England's Royal Shrine, the work of Our Lady and human hands *sauns fayle*.

8

Edith the Rich and Fair: Parentage and Family

THE CHRONOLOGICAL EVIDENCE and documentation detailing the birth and parentage of Edith the Fair is rudimentary, sometimes conflicting in detail, and fragmentary. However, we can build upon the evidence that we have, especially those relating to the land-holding and jurisdictions recorded in the Domesday books. The holdings of Edith throughout East Anglia, but especially in Cambridgeshire, could only be the result of committal lands and jurisdiction passing to her from parents, most probably the estates of her father from whom she inherited. This implies that she was first-born and that any other offspring, male or female, did not succeed, or that most probably she was the only surviving child.

The extensive East Anglian estates centred upon Cambridgeshire clearly indicate that they were the holdings of a former earl, and this is supported by the evidence that Edith's mother, Wulfhilda, was married firstly to Ulfcytel and secondly to his opponent and victor in the battle of Assundan, Thorkell the Tall, in 1016. Between 1016 and 1021, when Canute exiled Thorkell to Denmark, he was the King's most trusted advisor and acted for him during this period signing as primary witness to many of the most important state documents issued by King Edward. On the death of Edmund in 1016, Canute assumed immediate control of England. He divided the kingdom into the four prevailing great earldoms. He himself took command of Wessex, subsequently passing the region to Godwin senior, the father of Harold Godwin. Thorkell was given command of East Anglia, Mercia went to Eadric and Northumbria to Erik. Thorkell probably had command of East Anglia before this date, taking over from Ulfcytel on his death. Thorkell was Canute's most loyal commander, and the proof of this is his remaining in East Anglia whilst the new King took his armies north, south and west to secure the realm. Thorkell ensured that there was no East Anglian rebellion supported from Scandinavia or Denmark, although in the previous decades the area had been a hotspot for aggressive invasion and fierce rebellion.

During this period of unease, following Canute's conquest, Thorkell was the King's most trusted man. He was named separately at Archbishops Lyfing's request by Canute, writing to Christ Church Canterbury, reaffirming privileges that had been granted previously, which subsequently were part of Edith the Fair's patrimony. He also appears at the top of the list of Canute's earls in the brotherhood registry at Thorney Abbey. In the Saint Edmund edition in the MS Bodley 297, Thorkell, with the Queen and Aelfwine are identified, as having urged Canute to restore the Abbey in 1020.[1]

Between 1019 and 1021, the King sent out an official proclamation during his travels in the kingdom, as follows:

> If anyone, ecclesiastic or layman, Dane or Englishman, is so presumptuous to defy Gods

> law and my royal authority or the secular law and of which he will not make amends and desist according to the direction of my Bishops, I then pray and also command Earl Thorkell, if he can, to cause the evil doer to do right, destroy him in the land or drive him out of the land, whether he be of high or low rank.[2]

Thorkell was at this time trusted by Canute, who was sometime accorded the self-proclaimed title of Emperor of much of Northern Europe and Scandinavia. However, it was about this time that Canute elected to become very much an English monarch and also a Christian. This change of emphasis, with regard to his faith and his allegiance to England, was at odds with a Jomsviking commander such as Thorkell the Dane. We therefore have a reported series of events, which culminate in the banishment of Thorkell to his homeland of Denmark.

The hypothesis that Edith the Fair was the daughter of Thorkell the Tall, as evidenced above, is also supported by the following. Her mother Wulfhilda was the daughter of Aethelred the Unready and the half-sister of King Edward the Confessor. If it was the case that Edith the Fair was the daughter of Ulfcytel, Wulfhida's first husband who died at the battle of Assandun in 1016, she would have been between 26 and 29 years old on her marriage to Harold in 1042/5. Further, she would not have inherited the vast committal lands in Cambridgeshire and other counties in East Anglia. Her mother's will, described above, would have included her in the usual manner as the youngest daughter with her full brothers, Aelfketel and Ketel, as heirs to the land-holdings. It is reasonable to conclude that, as the daughter of Thorkell the Tall, brought up in the King's court, she became acquainted with Harold, and, as a niece of King Edward the Confessor, was shielded from the wrath of the Conqueror whose loyalty to Edward was the cornerstone of his claim to the English throne.

It is recorded by a clerk of Ramsay Abbey that Bishop Aelthric of Dorchester brought a case against Thorkell and his new wife, after a witch had confessed that she had been the wife's accomplice in the murder of Thorkell's son by his first marriage. Thorkell rejected the charges on behalf of himself and his wife. They were commanded to take an oath in order to establish their innocence before eleven peers at a place chosen by the bishop. He chose the place where the murdered child was buried. The Abbot of Ramsay attended, bringing sacred relics on which the oath had to be sworn. Thorkell swore his innocence and swore also on his beard on behalf of his wife, as was the Danish custom.

Astonishingly, the clerk records that his beard fell off. This is clearly a misreading of the manuscript evidence, which is no longer in existence. It is most probable that the reading should be understood as referring to the plaintiff's demeanour, as in modern parlance, as 'his face fell' or 'he was shamefaced'. Thorkell's wife maintained her innocence and only broke down, it is said, when the bishop ordered the grave to be opened. The trial ended with Thorkell and his wife being convicted, of perjury on the part of Thorkell, and murder on the part of his wife. Thorkell was also found guilty of insulting the bishop by ignoring his summons in the first place, for which he was required to grant a piece of land to the bishop who donated it to Ramsay Abbey.

This account is an example of writing which has no evidential support and which is clearly set down to justify a sentence that was very much at odds with the seriousness of the sins and crimes alleged. It is probable that its main purpose was to justify the ownership by the Abbey of the piece of land originally owned by Thorkell the Tall given to the bishop in reparation and in turn passed to the Abbey. The narrative as recorded for this purpose is an exaggerated and fanciful account of a partially recorded procedure that was not fully understood by the scribal author.

The evidence implies the murder of a child by a previous marriage, which clearly would not affect the status of Thorkell or any of his offspring. We already know that Thorkell's wife had been married previously; it may also be true that Thorkell had been married before; however, the charge specifically says that it was Thorkell's wife who, with the aid of a witch, committed homicide at some secret place. This does not make sense, we have no record of Thorkell having any children at this time, and it is difficult to create a scenario where child-murder would benefit the spouse of such a prominent individual. Further, it is implied that the grave was near to Ramsay Abbey which is a long way from Dorchester. The citation of the accused's beard falling off is a typical misreading of the Latinised English legal records of this time. The phrase, so badly translated, should read that the accused was 'downcast and shamed of face', not that he lost his hirsute appearance. It is also inexplicable in such brutal times that out of the blue 'a witch' came forward to confess her own complicity in the murder of a nobleman's son.

Finally, the verdict is guilty and the sentence banishment: the outcome most favourable to King Canute.

Thorkell, his right-hand advisor and army commander, who was probably his Jomsviking mentor, went to Denmark, which was part of Canute's empire, where he could be relied upon to provide cover and advanced warning of invasion. He took with him a hostage of the King's family and left behind in the English court a child to be brought up and protected by the English Royal Court. The threat of a Danish uprising with Thorkell at the centre in England would have been nullified and the English establishment around Canute mollified and likely to be more supportive of his continuing reign. Within three years, Canute and Thorkell were reconciled and it is possible that Canute paid one last visit to Denmark to meet with his long-standing friend and ally. It is almost certain that, had Thorkell conceived a male heir, he would have succeeded to the lands of the earldom of East Anglia, having been a ward of court of Canute.

However, it is just as probable (although totally overlooked) that Thorkell left behind him his only surviving child, who was female. In fact, she was probably Edith the Fair, raised in the English court who succeeded upon the death of her father sometime between 1023 and 1042 when Edward succeeded to the throne of England and appointed Harold as Earl of East Anglia. Edward, on coming to the throne, would also have had to approve of the marriage of his possible ward, Edith, daughter of Thorkell, to Earl Harold. Most importantly she was his father King Aethelred's granddaughter and Edward's half-sister. This speculation is satisfactory in the light of the facts of the Domesday record and is commendable in the light of the factual chronology and various accounts of Aethelred's three marriages. It is a working hypothesis that will be tested as further evidence comes to light. It has the support of the extant records, as set out above.

From the abundant first-hand evidence Edith the Fair, known in her day as Edeva rich and fair, was the Lady of the Manor of Walsingham, wife of Harold II of England, Visionary of the Shrine of the Salutation and Annunciation. It provides a clear understanding of the Pynson Ballad title of 'Rychold': Edith was indeed rich and fair and is described as such in innumerable documents. This pious Anglo Saxon-Danish noblewoman can now be understood with other 'royal women', such as Saint Margaret of Scotland, Saint Bridget of Sweden and that great line of Anglo-Saxon queens and noblewomen with whom the English nation is adorned; she was a woman who married and raised a family, and then went on to lead others, men and women who fulfilled their lives in the courts and towns, convents and castles who provided for the orphaned and the poor, building hospitals and schools and exercising power and authority for the good of all. She was a woman of authority and great wealth who, through prayer and perseverance, carried out Our Lady's commands in founding the Royal Shrine of the Salutation. Edith was a visionary who loved much and provided England with its Holy House.

Notes

1 3358 Oxford, Bodleian library, MS Bodley297 [s.c.2468]. John of Worcester chronicle, down to 131, (Cambridge M.S.92).

2 King Cnut's proclamation letter to the people of England 1019–1020, in *York Gospels*, F. Lieberman (ed.) (Halle, 1903–1916), pp. 140–145.

9

The Prayer of Desiderius Erasmus

In 1511, one of the great European humanist scholars of the Renaissance, who had himself joined the Augustinian Canons in his youth as an orphan, and who had been subsequently ordained but without a real vocation and with some reluctance, reverted and was laicized sometime in his late twenties. It is probable that his mistaken vocation was a symptom of his bleak childhood: his mother died when he was still an infant and he was left in the care of the canons. He came to fulfil a vow which he had made to Our Lady of Walsingham in thanksgiving for her care and inspiration in his own much-troubled lifetime, which had been a great comfort to him. Like many devout and learned scholars, his devotion to the Mother of God was a lifelong commitment marked by daily prayer and fervent pilgrimage.

Erasmus was a considerable sceptic with regard to many aspects of medieval piety and the excesses of many pilgrims in the veneration of Holy relics, some of which were clearly manufactured for the sake of gain which bordered upon simony. He also recognised that the gullibility of many pilgrims was innocent of deliberate deception and required of the clergy much greater rigour in instruction of the faithful. He urged reform and education, and had no sympathy with Luther or his English counterpart's reforms, which were often a denial of scriptural and sacramental truth.

He combined his visit to the Shrine with a lengthy stay at the University of Cambridge, where it is believed he carried out some teaching and tutoring responsibilities. The Augustinian Canons were themselves regular clergy who, together with taking part in the daily office, were renowned as scholars who taught locally and sponsored the most able pupils to the colleges that were part of university organisation in places such as Ely, Lynn, Norwich and Cambridge. Erasmus was an eminent classical scholar and had composed some Greek verses for Our Lady which he presented to Our Lady of the Annunciation and Salutation as his offering at the Shrine of Walsingham Priory.

Erasmus wrote from Cambridge to his close collaborator and friend, Andreas Ammonius, that this offering as a scholar would be appreciated by the guardians of the Shrine and was offered in honour of Our Lady, recalling the New Testament of the Septuagint. These verses were preserved in copies of his work, collected in 1540 by his colleague Frobenius. He also, in about 1530, wrote a satire lampooning the interrogatory processes of the reformation zealots with regard to their mistaken belief in the ignorance and stupidity of the canons. His satire on the perverted misunderstanding of these so-called commissioners was subsequently controverted and used by them as a commentary on the failings of the Shrine's guardians.

The canons were well schooled in the Classics and undoubtedly would have delighted in and much appreciated Erasmus' work in honour of Our Blessed Lady.

The following verses of Erasmus have been rendered in English and have subsequently lost some of the innate beauty and many-splendored meaning of the original text, in their complexity of meaning and allusion to classical and ancient mythology.

The prayer of Erasmus

'Hail' Jesus' mother, blessed evermore
Alone of women God-bearing and virgin
Others may offer thee various gifts
This man his gold, that man his silver
A third adorn thy shrine with precious stones
Some ask for the bounty of good health
Some riches, others hope by thy aid
They soon may bear a father's honoured name
Or gain the learning of Pylus' revered sage
But the poor poet for his well-meant song
Bringing these verses all he has
Asks in reward for his humble gift
The greatest blessing; piety of heart
And full remission for his many sins.[1]

Thus we hear a great scholar of his time, having travelled over land and sea, making his humble pilgrim's petition, offering Our Lady of Walsingham his skill as a poet and man of learning and asking for the reward from the Mother of God, of piety of heart and forgiveness for his many sins. This demonstrates the beauty and humble faith of the medieval church of the House of Tudor and that great line of English monarchs that stretches back to Alfred the Great. Erasmus was one of the most renowned scholars of his day, and there can be no doubt whatsoever that he believed in the efficacy and miraculous foundation of the Shrine that was of course already over four hundred years old when he made his pilgrimage. Erasmus was a man of the enlightenment and was sceptical of many of the practices that had arisen over indulgences, the wealth and corruption of some bishoprics and abbacies and the corruption of benefices accruing to persons of little piety and in deprivation of the poor and needy. He was a critic of corruption and simony. It is all the more remarkable that he remained convinced of the wonder and efficacy of the Shrine of Our Lady of Walsingham. His prayer, written in Greek, is a profound gift, expressing love and loyalty to Our Blessed Lady and the great powers of her intercession.

In the twentieth century, we still write our prayers and petitions and the Royal Taper still burns in witness, reminding us of the Holy presence of the Spirit of Joy that comes down upon us at the Salutation and Annunciation, when Mary the Virgin humbly requested, "that it should be done unto her according to thy Word". We are reminded as we attend upon her in the Manor of Walsingham that England is Her dowry and that we are invited to the wedding feast, as we journey from the highways and the byways of this world rejoicing, that one day we will don our wedding garments and join the guests, where Jesus Her son is the bridegroom and the law of love is fully revealed.

The Walsingham statue of Our Lady was copied from the original medieval seal now in the care of the British Museum. It shows Our Lady seated on the throne of Wisdom, crowned in the manner of Anglo-Saxon monarchs; imagery which draws us to him with the work of human hands as Christ the King. This iconographic image is the sign of the revelation of Christ's Incarnation; He is King of all Creation.

Jesus is seated on Our Lady's left knee, offering to all the good news of the New Testament, The Living Word.

The Mother of God holds in her right hand the flowering branch of the Tree of Jesse, thus revealing for us the 'Flower of Nazareth': Jesus the messiah, and the branch of the tree of life and the vine of redemption, His mother. The seven-banded scroll around the uprights of Our Lady's throne of Wisdom reveals the Seven Sacraments, through which redemption is offered by his Church here on Earth. This iconographic display of the Seven Sacraments also dates the Shrine to the early eleventh century to the time of the promulgation of the canonical teaching of the Sacrament of Marriage in 1055.

Thus we are reminded of the prophecy of Isaiah, 11 1-9. This messianic psalm reveals the splendid details of the coming of the Davidic Messiah. He will be filled with the spirit of the prophets, and He will establish a society of integrity revealing God's sanctity here on Earth. He will restore the peace of Eden, which is the fruit of the knowledge of God, face to face. This is the Old Testament fulfilled in the presence of the Mother of God as announced by the Angel Gabriel. At Walsingham, too, Our Lady of the Salutation and Annunciation, the Infant Jesus is brought to us through the language of iconography as the Messiah to which Our Lady gives Her woman's witness. Through Her we are lead to Him, Our Saviour, in the New and Everlasting Covenant.

Isaiah, chapter 11, v. 1–5

A shoot will spring from the stock of Jesse
A new shoot will grow from its roots
On him will rest the Spirit of Yahweh
The spirit of wisdom and insight
The spirit of counsel and power
The spirit of knowledge and fear of Yahweh
His inspiration will lie in fearing Yahweh
His judgements will not lie in appearances

His verdict not based on hearsay
He will judge the weak with integrity
And give fair sentence to the humblest in the land
He will strike the country with the rod of his mouth
And with the breath of his lips bring death to the wicked
Uprightness will be the belt around his waist
And constancy the belt upon his hips.

These are the prayers and lessons which flow from the Shrine and Seal of Our Lady of Walsingham, where the house of the Salutation at Nazareth was transported and set down in Norfolk, England, Her Dowry. This work was accomplished through the visions of Edith and the work of her artificers, creating a place where the saints could rejoice and sinners take refuge.

Thus we understand the iconography through medieval cognitive perceptions, informing the onlooker not in purely linguistic terms, but with much wider and more complex human responses, using a combination of iconic illustrations and signs, including colour, design, pattern and reference to oral text to fully illuminate the majesty of Our Lady's presence within the house of the Salutation at Nazareth. This is the childlike attitude with which we come into the Kingdom of God that underlines all the teaching of the Gospel: "Unless you become like one of these children, you shall not enter into the Kingdom." This has oft-times been judged naive and ingenuous and has been mistaken as ignorance, especially by the learned and sceptical intelligentsia. The artistic message combined with intellectual evaluation and appreciation requires a complete human involvement that leads us from observers (that is, a passive audience): from beholding the form extended, and acting, into tasting and hearing the substance of living prayer in the embrace of an All-Loving God. The embrace is tactile and fully human, heart speaking to heart. This is the medieval understanding of the pilgrim rejoicing on the pilgrimage. A fully human response to God Incarnate, he dwells with us and Nazareth is the home of his conception, "The Word Made Flesh that dwells among us".

The fully human response has become filtered and distorted through the 'scientific' speciality lens, which fails to evaluate data in its contextual and holistic dimensions of human limitations, yet without limitation in the soaring response of imagination and spiritual awareness. This is over and against empirical enquiry, whereby knowledge is locked into an esoteric language and remains unknown as simple natural phenomena, savoured by the children of the Incarnation. The medieval-Christian pilgrim journeyed to the Shrine, which signified the divine in action in the living body of Christ His Church. Thus, the message to all through the Walsingham seals and sacramental, prayers and hopes is simple in its vast complexity. God became incarnate of the Virgin Mary for our salvation, in all the beauty of the Creed, leaving the Good News forever with us, which we must receive like little children sitting upon the knee of Mary His mother. The gifts we ask of Her are the same as that great scholar Erasmus: we ask that our sins be forgiven, and for piety of heart.

Notes

1 *Victoria County History, Norfolk*, vol. 2, W. Page (ed.) (London: Boydell & Brewer, 1906), p. 42.

10

Gunhild, Royal Daughter of the Convent of Wilton

GUNHILD WAS PROBABLY in early puberty when she was sent to the royal convent at Wilton, whose royal patron was Queen Edith, wife of King Edward. It was a convent where her mother Edith the Fair sometimes resided and Gunhilda was probably an honoured guest and provisional novice. My chronology, whereby Edith her mother was born *c.* 1018–25 together with a marriage to Earl Harold in 1042–45 gives us her mother's age range in 1093 as in her late sixties. Assuming that Gunhilda was born in her mother's thirtieth year or thereabouts, the timescale is in line with other evidence; at the time of the Conquest she would have been in her early teenage years and probably did not have at that time a vocation.

Count Alan the Red of Brittany was a very rich, powerful and important independent supporter of William the Conqueror; he was his son-in-law and ranked third in the hierarchy of the Norman Magnates. All of Edith the Rich and Fair's land-holdings were given to him and there is an obvious important bond of fealty between the Count and Edith and Harold. This bond may have been formed on Harold's diplomatic mission in 1062–3 and there is evidence that connects Harold as saving a member of the Count's family from certain death in a quicksand episode recorded on the Bayeux Tapestry. Gunhilda, being underage, was technically abducted by Count Alan; however, in the event of her refusal to return to the convent we may reflect that she was probably a very willing escapee and enjoyed the protection and attention of one of the most rich and powerful magnates under the new regime. Count Alan the Red died soon after the abduction and Gunhilda immediately either married or openly lived with his younger brother, Count Alan the Black. Her mother's extensive estates in East Anglia, inherited from the very formidable Thorkell the Tall of Denmark appear to have remained the property of Gunhild and were much coveted by King William II. Had she returned to the convent as a novice or professed sister, she would have taken vows of poverty and the lands inherited from her mother would have reverted to King William II. This is one reason why so much pressure was applied through Archbishop Anselm to persuade her to return to Wilton. She was adamant that she had not taken her final vows and therefore only pious persuasion was open to Anselm.

The letter from Archbishop Anselm is a genuine and eloquent statement, beautifully drafted with great skill, understanding and compassion and expressing a very clear and deep appreciation of the nature and wonder of human heterosexual love. It is also important evidence that links Gunhild as daughter of Edith the Fair and Harold, supported by the evidence of the Domesday Book for Cambridge whereby her landholdings are placed under the royal jurisdiction of Count Alan of Brittany.

I have therefore included the letter from Archbishop Anselm for two distinct purposes; first, it shows how important a royal princess the daughter of Edith the Fair and King Harold was. Second, it demonstrates the high degree of skill and care that was brought to bear on this issue of Edith's land-holdings and the crucial role of the royal convent of Wilton.

> Anselm, by the ordination of God, archbishop of Canterbury, to his beloved sister and daughter, Gunhild, daughter of King Harold. According to the flesh, wishing that she may scorn the world, not Christ[,] and love Christ more than the world.
>
> I would most gladly speak to you if I could; sister of mine truly beloved in God, since the charity by which I wish all men to be saved and the office laid upon me require me to love you with fraternal and paternal affection[,] showing solicitude for the salvation of your soul because of that overwhelming love. As we have no opportunity for talking together circumstances require me to write of my thoughts for you and what I most dearly long for your heartsease.
>
> I ask humbly that you do not spurn the love I have for you for the sake of Our Lord, for the honour of God and for your own salvation, for this alone do not reject this advice. If you are moved to agree with me never doubt that you will be full of joy at your end. There will also be great joy among all the angels watching over you. If you however choose not to do so know well that you will be troubled in your heart and that you will have no defence before His sorrowing judgement. I have heard beloved sister that you wore the habit of holy monastic

life for a long time. How you divested yourself and suffered and the accompanying circumstances are well known.

Consider[,] ponder and recall how small and unworthy are the embraces of men and the pleasures of this world from the embraces of Christ. From the indelible pleasures of chastity and the purity of your burning heart are loving gifts offered to Jesus. I do not describe the embraces of Christ as physical, they are such that unites your soul as an intimate friend through love and desire joined and formed in conscience as lovers of love. I ask you to carefully consider these two forms of pleasure. I am not now speaking of lawful marriage. How great is the immensity of spiritual pleasure, compared to the impurity of carnal pleasures. Recall what the spiritual promises and what the carnal threatens. How much Hope there is in the spiritual[,] how much delightful expectation to be united in Christ. Recall in the spiritual[,] even in this life[,] the joy in anticipation[,] how much security and consolation. In carnal pleasure, how great the fear and shame[,] even in this life of just judgement.

Contemplate what it means to scorn Christ your spouse, who promises you the Kingdom of Heaven as your dowry. To prefer a man to the Son of God, the King of Kings to a mortal man who can offer only corruption and the contemptible things of this world. Indeed this King of Kings has desired your beauty as his spouse[:] in what ways[,] my sister[,] can any mortal man grasp your beauty? Most noble woman[,] how can it be said? You[,] a virgin chosen to be a spouse of God, marked out for him in the delight of your flesh[,] your habit and your way of life.

What has now come to pass with you? My daughter[,] I do not speak of this in order to take pleasure in your shame but rather that I should be overcome with joy at your repentance and that God rejoices and the Angels with Him. What do I say? If I say; nothing perhaps then you will not notice, if I do speak perhaps you will be angry. What have you done with the chosen one, you the designated spouse of God? Your nobility is offended; you may bridle and blush at what you hear. I am sore afraid to offend you but behold dearest daughter[,] if you face these facts how great must be the grief in your heart at this most grave and serious fall. If you grieve deeply I will grieve with you, and yet rejoice over you. If you do not grieve then there will only be grief for me[:] no rejoicing[,] only grief. If you grieve then there is Hope in your salvation, if you do not grieve there is the prospect of the desolation of damnation.

It is impossible to be saved unless you return to the habit and the vowed life. Even though you were not consecrated by the Bishop and did not read your vows in his presence these vows were implicit and it is not denied that you wore the habit. Showing your holy intention in both private and public actions. In this you demonstrated to everyone who saw you that you were dedicated to God[,] though you did not read out your vows. Before the now common profession of vows and consecration to monastic life was required many showed by wearing the habit that that they were manifesting this desired intention. Through this posture they demonstrated that they were pursuing the sublimely the Crown of

> Glory. Those then who subsequently rejected the habit were adjudged apostates. Therefore you may be without excuse if you desert your holy intention, with which you wore the habit and displayed this way of life.
>
> Surely dearest daughter your Lord and Creator and Redeemer, is waiting for you who desires you in your beauty[.] He is calling you back so that you may be his glorious bride. If not a virgin; chaste[,] for we know of many holy women who having lost their virginity were more pleasing to God and closer to him through penitence and their chastity than many others even though they were virgins.
>
> Return then Christian woman[,] return to your heart, consider whom you should choose, to whom should you cleave. The one who chooses you for such honour and who called you, who waits for you calling you back, even though he has been scorned and rejected.[1]

The letter concludes with these lines: 'May Almighty God visit your heart and pour into you his love dearest daughter. I ask you to let me know by letter how you received this paternal letter of mine.'

In this letter by the Archbishop, we have a clear indication of a number of important facts. He writes with great deference to the lady Gunhild, addressing her as a member of the royal nobility and referring to her father as King Harold. This indicates that in some ecclesiastical circles, at a high level, Harold's crowning was legitimate. This regal identity is supported more clearly when it is accepted that Gunhild was the granddaughter of King Aethelred and that her mother, Edith the Fair, was the wife of King Harold II. Further, the 'abduction', if that is what it was, from Wilton convent, was known to her mother. Also, that the third most important magnate of the Norman dynasty, Count Alan of Brittany, son-in-law of the Conqueror would not have been associated with any but the most noble rich and powerful English lady. This, then, supports the understanding that her mother was Edith the Fair, wife of Harold and Visionary of Walsingham.

As shown above, the Visionary of Walsingham was a devout Christian lady and through her mother Wulfhilda directly related to King Edward the Confessor. She was the wife of King Harold and daughter of the greatest warrior and Danish magnate of those turbulent times. Yet the greatest of all her deeds was to carry out the commands of Our Blessed Lady of the Salutation and continue the wonderful line of Anglo-Saxon queens and kings of England, which continues through the House of Windsor to this day.

Notes

1 *Sancti Anselmi Cantuariensis Archiepiscopi, Opera Omnia,* F.S. Schmitt (ed.) (Edinburgh: T. Nelson, 1946–63). Translation from *The Letters of Saint Anselm of Canterbury,* trans. Walter Fröhlich, Cistercian Studies 97, 3v (Kalamazoo: Cistercian Publications, 1990–94).

11

Princess Gytha, Wife of Monomakh

Gytha is named as Harold's daughter in the Fagriskinna, which later records unambiguously that she married 'Vladimir Konongr sun larozlaeifs konongs I Holmegarde'.[1]

After her father's death, Gytha and two brothers immediately made their way to Denmark, where Svend II Erithson, King of Denmark, received them into the embrace of his family: 'Their famed father Thorkell the Tall, of Jomsberg striding over the seas to greet them'.[2] This record of the Saga uses the language of the Broderbund and implies that, although Thorkell the Tall was dead, he inhabited the worlds of Valhalla.

King Erithson gave Gytha in marriage to Waldemarus, King of the Russians: the Grand Prince Vladimir Monomakh. This is contrary to some commentators who have stated that Gytha was not considered a suitable marriage partner due to her 'illegitimate status and from an obscure Lineage'.[3] These assumptions I have shown above to be incorrect. Gytha's mother Edith was the daughter of the Jomsviking Thorkell the Tall and Wulfhilda (her grandmother), the daughter of King Aethelred of England. Her husband under Danish law was Harold II of England: thus Gytha would have been highly suitable for such a marriage at this time.

Vladimir II Monomakh was one of the most famous rulers of Kievan Rus. Gytha was thus the mother of Mstislav the Great, renowned as the ruler of the united Kievan Rus and celebrated as a great warrior, yet Christian father who wrote some wonderful letters full of advice and Christian compassion to his court and children. Gytha was mother to at least five children by Vladimir Monomakh and in the Norse sagas Mstislav their eldest son is called Harald after his grandfather, which supports the evidence and conclusions above. The pateric inscriptions in the Saint Pantaleon Cloister in Cologne state that 'Gytha the Queen' died as a nun on 10th March. She probably went with Geoffrey de Bouillon on the first or second crusade, died and was buried in Palestine. She would of course have been fully aware of the Walsingham visions from her mother and like many pious men and women from all classes at this time made her way to the Holy Lands to be united with Christ in His birthplace, and at Calvary, where He died to save us all. Her death probably occurred about 1098, a year before Vladimir married another woman.

The other children of this famous marriage were also renowned in their day, as follows: Isyaslav Vladimirovich, Prince of Kursk (died 6 September 1096); Syatoslav Vladimirovich, Prince of Smolensk and Pereyslav (died 6 March 1114); Yaropolk II Kiev (died 18 February 1139); and Viacheslav I of Kiev (died 2 February 1154). It is reported that, as a result of this union of Harold's daughter to Monomakh, our present Queen Elizabeth through her European ancestry is the thirty-second niece of King Harold, and from there her illustrious lineage can be traced to her renowned predecessor, Alfred the Great. In addition, her consort the Duke of Edinburgh's ancestry can also be traced to King Harold of the House of Wessex.

Notes

1 A. Nazarenko, *Древняя Русь на международных путях* (Moscow: Русский фонд содействия образованию и науке, 2001). For the benefit of non-Russian-speaking readers, the title translates literally as *'Old Rus on international roads', published in English as International Relations of Ancient Rus.* The publisher is the Russian foundation for co-operation in science and research.

2 M. J. Trow, *Cnut, Emperor of the North* (Stroud: Sutton, 2005), pp. 44–57.

3 N. Lund, 'Danish Empire and the end of the Viking age' in *The Oxford Illustrated History of the Vikings*, P. H. Sawyer (ed.) (Oxford: Oxford University Press, 2001), pp. 167–181.

12

Three Christian Kings

This chapter sets out the relationship between three kings, two of whom—Edward the Confessor and Canute—dominated the consolidation of the English nation in the first 65 years of the eleventh century. The third, King Harold, was indeed mentored by King Edward, and his father Earl Godwin was very much the great Anglo-Saxon supporter of King Canute. These relationships were bound up in the Christian ideals of kingship, and although Canute was known as Emperor of the North (that is England and the British Isles and the Scandinavian countries), he lived his final decade as King of the British Isles and was baptised a Christian. Their lives were all linked and influenced by the Holy Cross of Waltham. This ancient Holy Cross was recovered from a buried cache of very early Romano-British artefacts, many of which had very clear Christian origins. This find was very important in the life of King Canute. It was found by his standard bearer, Tovi the Proud, who was at the time shire reeve of Somerset under the old Anglo-Saxon system. It was taken to Waltham by Epping Forest, by command of the King. Waltham was an ancient British settlement on the banks of the River Lea and therefore of great importance in the defence of the Thames Estuary and the City of London.

The cartularies of the abbey refer to a foundation chapel dedicated to Saint Laurence (see above), which supports an early date for Waltham as a Christian site, because dedication of chapels to Saint Laurence were widespread among the English nobility from the early fourth century. This black-flint cross, because of its size and colouring, was considered to have originated from Brittany, from whence of course Britain was first converted by Christian merchants, sailors and soldiers from this northern department of France, or Gaul as it was then called. Found in the heart of ancient Wessex, it was considered a sign of a new standard, a Christian sacramental that moved King Canute to accept conversion. This was not a standard to be displayed in battle, but a sign of the Holy Cross of love and redemption. The Cross was venerated in the church built especially for it at Waltham and became a place of prayer and pilgrimage for many.

On his succession to the throne, King Edward the Confessor granted the Church and other lands to Harold, whom he made Earl of East Anglia, and allowed him to marry Edith the Fair, only known child and daughter of Thorkell the Tall, counsellor of King Canute, who bequeathed to Edith the vast committal lands of Ulfcytel and also his own holdings in the year 1060 (a year prior to the founding of the Holy Shrine of Walsingham by Edith). Harold was struck down by paralysis and cured through prayers offered by him and others before the Holy Cross. The church was then rebuilt by him and dedicated to Saint Laurence and the Holy Cross on 3rd May 1060 in thanksgiving for Harold's recovery. This was five years before King Edward completed the rebuilding of Westminster Abbey. Harold also founded a college at Waltham Cross of Austin Canons with eleven canons and a dean. A century or so later, the Austin Canons was granted the guardianship of the Shrine of Our Lady of Walsingham.

King Harold, on his journey south, to confront the invader William at the battle of Hastings, stopped for the night to pray before the Holy Cross to prepare his soul for battle. The Austin Canons continued on this site until 1177, when as part of his penance for the murder of Archbishop Thomas a Becket, Henry II founded a much larger abbey on the site, for the Augustinian order whose professed abbot took his place in parliament. Waltham Abbey Church is considered by some (although this is much disputed by eminent authorities) to be the burial place of King Harold. In my considered view, this is improbable, as we have good evidence that Harold's body was mutilated on the battlefield and was therefore unrecognisable.

There are, of course, many secondary sources written a century or more after these events which claim identification by Harold's wife. This is not feasible, and contrary to this his mother offered his weight in gold in exchange for his body, which the Conqueror refused. Edith the Fair, wife of Harold, left England between 1066 and 1070, with her second-youngest daughter, Gytha, and her great desire was to visit the Holy Land and the Holy House of Nazareth. There is evidence from continental contemporary sources and a memorial in Cologne Cathedral that she set out to make this pilgrimage, but there is no evidence of her completing the journey. The evidence in support of this narrative demonstrates the series of events from King Canute through Edward the Confessor to King Harold, which supports the understanding of Harold's trust in ecclesiastical matters directed by Edward and their shared faith in the most important matters of ecclesiastical veneration.

This shared devotion for the very important Abbey of Waltham and the place of the Holy Cross in royal circles of this time was significant. Waltham Abbey was, from the time of King Canute to Henry VIII, a most important royal shrine and one of the last to be suppressed in the reign of Henry VIII. Thus three kings are brought together at the close of the Anglo-Saxon line of British kings. This royal Anglo-Saxon line is remarkable for its many saints, martyrs and confessors, its close links and ties with the Roman patriarchs and with the Royal Shrine of Our Lady of Walsingham. In this time of the House of Windsor, the ancient churches of Rome, the East and the Anglican community reside together in a great ecumenical gathering of Our Lady of Walsingham.

Summary and Conclusions

The Domesday records for the Manor of Walsingham show beyond all reasonable doubt that before 1066, this manor belonged to Earl Harold, later King of England, who died at the Battle of Hastings in 1066. His wife, Edith Swanneshals, known also as Rychold or rich and fair, lived with Harold in various locations in East Anglia, one of which was the Manor of Walsingham adjacent to Great and Little Walsingham, manors held by her half-brothers, Ulfketel and Ketel; this is confirmed in the last will and testament of their mother, Wulfgyth, which was witnessed by none other than King Edward the Confessor (see below). Harold in 1061 was Earl of Wessex, having succeeded his father, although he was not the oldest son. Previously, as Earl of East Anglia appointed by King Edward the Confessor, he resided close to the King's own holdings in Norfolk in the Hundred of North Greenhow, which include the important port of Wells on Sea. Harold's place of administration, including the Royal Assize, was the nearby ancient British-Romano settlement and then Scandinavian borough of Fakenham. The Walsingham Manorial Holding of Harold and Edith were assessed as an outlier of the borough of Fakenham.

The Domesday Book provides a wealth of information regarding land value and ownership, before and after 1066, and the detail of the agricultural and commercial economy including tithes due and the many trades and lawful enterprises against a varied background of church and royal jurisdictions. These include taxes, tribute, jurisdiction and many aspects of manorial, town and village occupation. The Manor of Walsingham in 1061 at the time of the Shrine's foundation would have been one of the homes of Harold's wife, Edith the Fair, with adjacent properties in Great and Little Walsingham held by her half-brothers, Ulfketel and Ketel; as sons of Ulfketel Snoring they also held Great Snoring in the Greenhow Hundred. Thus we began our researches to understand in greater detail the person Rychold, the visionary of the Pynson Ballad, about whom we now have evidence that support the understanding that she is the Walsingham visionary who was also the wife of Harold, Lord of this Manor, who was according to the charters of Edward the Confessor, Earl of East Anglia and later King of England.

As above, we demonstrate that Edith the Fair was born in the reign of King Canute. She was most probably the daughter of Thorkell the Tall, Earl of East Anglia, first advisor to King Canute and famous Danish warrior. Her mother was Wulfhilda (sometimes known as Wulfgyth), daughter of King Aethelred, and Edith the Fair as recorded in the Cambridge Domesday succeeded her father in extensive land-holdings throughout the county and throughout East Anglia, which had been held by Ulfketel Snillingri, the first husband of Wulfhilda. These holdings in Cambridge were committal lands, previously belonging to the famous Anglo-Saxon warrior Ulfcytel, who appears to have been slain by Thorkell the Tall at the Battle of Ashington.

When Thorkell was expelled from England and banished to Denmark by King Edward, they exchanged hostages and it may have been at this time that Edith remained in England as a ward of court of King Canute. Earl Godwin became Canute's first advisor and his second son, Harold, would then have met Edith the Fair at the king's court in Winchester and Canterbury.

On the death of King Canute, after much uncertainty, Edward the Confessor was consecrated King of England and very early in his reign he married Earl Godwin's daughter, Edith, appointed Harold Godwin as Earl of East Anglia and sanctioned the marriage of Harold to Edith the Fair. Edith retained all her land and jurisdictions and burgess tenement holdings in Cambridge and elsewhere on the death of her father Thorkell the Tall. The King granted land, especially in the southern parts of East Anglia, to Harold as part of the earldom confirmed as the king's gift on the appointment of a new Earl.

The marriage of Harold and Edith the Fair was carried through according to the Danish custom, as was her father's marriage to Wulfhilda and Canute's marriages; this form of hand-fast marriage was favoured by the nobility at a time when the men often died before they were 45 and their noblewomen married two or three times, or elected to retire to one of the famous royal monasteries, where they lived as they wished in tranquillity, yet wielded great influence and were protected from the slaughter and savagery that created so many widows, orphans and fatherless families amongst the ruling elite. The references to a hand-fast marriage designated 'illegitimate' are largely from secondary sources hostile to Harold. There is, then, a likelihood from the evidence that both Harold and Edith the Fair, who were devout Christians, were married in the church according to the Sacramental Order of Christian marriage, as well as being married in the Danish manner; there is no evidence of such a marriage, although both Harold and Edith were close to Archbishop Stigand and Harold to Saint Wulfstan, Bishop of Worcester.

For the whole of Edward's 24-year reign, Harold and Edith had a happy and settled marriage with a blessing of six children; they were, the evidence suggests, both devout Christians and shared a special devotion to the saint and Roman martyr, Laurence.

Following the death of Harold in 1066, Our Lady's Shrine at Walsingham remained in royal ownership. It was the focus until the time of Henry III of local devotion, with semi-royal status in the Anglo-Saxon tradition, but became famous for its Royal patronage at the time of Edward the Confessor, only in the reign of the Plantagenets. It was the Chapel of Henry VII's personal banner used at the decisive battle of Stoke, displayed in thanksgiving for his most famous and final victory, which brought an end to the War of the Roses, the conflict between the Houses of York and Lancaster; truly a victory of great significance. This famous victory united the Houses of Lancaster and York and confirmed the prosperity and unity of England under the reign of the House of Tudor.

From the time of King Canute until *c.* 1150, there was almost a century and a half of regional strife, invasion from the Scandinavian countries and northern Europe and rebellion in England, apart from the 22-year reign of King Edward and the firm rule of William II. This turbulence was partly resolved as Britain became a consolidated nation under one Sovereign Lord with distinct regional earls, established by ancient custom.

The Shrine's date of foundation in 1061, in the reign of King Edward, has never been challenged by any well-informed commentator. The date is confirmed in the Pynson Ballad commissioned by Henry VII and validated by John Leland (appointed by his successor, King Henry VIII). The detailed LDB record of 1086 confirms that throughout the reigns of William II and the Angevin dynasty, the shrine was a royal holding, held at one time by 'Geoffrey'. That this royal land-holding was in the jurisdiction of the high sheriffs appointed by William the Conqueror is confirmed by the signatures of their successors, acting for the King in the reign of Henry II when the Shrine passed to the Bishopric of Norwich to be administered by the canons. Thus, as the royal Shrine from 1066, it is inconceivable that it could have been founded in the time of the Norman or Angevin dynasties. William II left some wealthy episcopal appointments vacant wherever he could divert church revenues to his exchequer and his interest in ecclesiastical matters other than as sources of wealth was minimal. The upheaval and civil wars that took place during the dispute between Matilda and Stephen cannot reasonably be considered a time conducive to such a Shrine's foundation.

There can be no reasonable doubt that the Shrine was founded in 1061, as attested by the oral tradition of the Pynson Ballad; the printed edition by the King's Printer underlines this date. It is significant that the Shrine was left as the King's land-holding under the guardianship of the royal tenants such as Geoffrey sometime after 1088. The founding of the Shrine during the reign of King Edward had never been challenged until the nineteenth century. The date of the replica Holy House was never questioned, despite enquiries that purported to show that the repair and maintenance through the centuries had been carried out. This is confirmed by the removal of the house to London where it was burnt, which would have been unnecessary in the event that the 'commissioners' had found a fraudulent relic constructed later. Further, the bearskin adornment of the Chapel would have been a costly and high-status gift that would have had a date retained and commemorated in local tradition. The bearskin was a royal accoutrement and would have had the high status associated with a royal foundation. It is therefore possible that it was given to the Shrine by King Edward in honour of Our Blessed Lady and the Shrine's visionary founder, his great-niece.

The accuracy and fidelity of oral traditions of this nature has been proved in their fundamentals as astonishingly precise in terms of dating and other provenance. The bearskin, then, would have been a royal gift, and its fame as such would firmly fix the date as recalled as a foundation of the time of King Edward the Confessor. It is also of great importance that the statue is understood as a very early form of the teaching of Mary as descended from King David. She is crowned and holds the flowering stem of the Tree of Jesse, towards which the Infant Jesus on her left knee points. This form of iconic teaching is without question from the early eleventh century and categorically cannot be dated to the twelfth. I therefore conclude that the Visionary founder of the Walsingham Shrine was Edith Rychold Swanneshals, wife of King Harold who died at Hastings, and that the significance of the Shrine is indicated through the ancient iconography, which reveals that Jesus the Messiah is truly Man from the royal lineage of Mary, His mother, fecundated by the Holy Spirit without the aid of mortal man.

The Wulfgyth Charter (Christ Church)

The following passage is taken from *The Charters of Christ.*[1] This is the will of her described as Wulfgyth, which is also transcribed as Wulfhilda AD 1044 x 1053, possibly dated to 1046. These dates coincide with the Confessor's reign from 1042 to 1066 and probably the marriage of Harold and Edith the Fair and Rich in 1044/6. Wulfhilda's first husband, Ulfcytel, died in the battle of Assandun in 1016 and the Jomsviking victor who was Cnut's commander-in-chief, Thorkell Havi, subsequently married Wulfhilda. He then sired his daughter, Edith Swanneshals the rich and fair (and subsequently the wife of Harold, who was appointed Earl of East Anglia in 1045). It is against this background and understanding that we have some insight into the will of Wulfgyth/Wulfhilda.

The translation taken from the Charters of Christ Church is as follows:

> Here is made known in this document how after her demise Wulfgyth will bestow her things. Of which Almighty God has allowed her to enjoy the use of in life,
>
> That is to my Lord his due heriot. And I grant the estate at Stisted [Essex] with the witness of God and my friends, to Christ Church for the support of the monks on condition that Aelfketel and Ketel, my children, may have the

use of the estate in their day, and afterwards the estate is to pass to Christ Church without any controversy for my soul and my lord Aelfwine's and for the souls of all my children and after their day half the men [dependants] are to be free. And to the church in Stisted, besides what I gave in my lifetime, I grant *Eldemesland* and so much in addition that there shall be in all fifty acres of woodland and open country after my demise. And I grant to Ulfketel [presumably meaning Ulfketel] and Ketel my sons, the estates at Walsingham [in east Carleton] and east Carleton and at [East] Harling [all Norfolk]. And I grant to my two daughters, Gode and Bote, Saxlingham [Norfolk]. And Somerleyton [or Somerton, both Suffolk] and to the church at Somerleyton [or Somerton] sixteen acres of [arable] land and one acre of meadow. And I grant to Ealdgyth, my daughter, the estates at Chadacre [Suffolk] and at *Essetesford* and the wood, which I attached thereto. And I grant Fritton [Suffolk?] to Earl Godwine and Earl Harold [Note Harold was made Earl in 1045 which points to a date for this will of 1045/6]. And I grant for Christ Church for Christ's altar a little golden crucifix and a seat cover. And I grant to St. Edmunds's [Bury] two ornamental horns. And I grant to St. Aelthryth's [Ely] a purple or [costly] garment. And I grant to St. Oswyth's half a pound in cash and my children are to pay that. And I grant to St. Augustine's one dorsal.

And let him who may diminish my will, which I now have made known in the witness of God, have his joy on earth diminished, and may Almighty God who created and made all creatures, exclude him from the fellowship of the

> Saints on the day of Judgement. And may he be delivered into the abysm of hell to Satan the Devil and all his accursed companions and there suffer with God's opponents without end, and [may he] never afflict my heirs.
>
> Of this King Edward and many others are witness.

Thus King Edward's sister or half-sister calls upon him as witness, and this charter will binds together the Families of Wulfgyth, Harold and Edith in a specific relation to the King and Christ's Church at Canterbury, and also to the Manors of Walsingham which is confirmed by the LDB 1088.

Notes

1 N. P. Brookes and S. E. Kelly (eds.), *Charters of Christ Church Canterbury* (Oxford: Oxford University Press, 2013), number 176.

Appendix A

The Godwin Family's Holding and Thorkell the Tall

Taken from the Domesday Book Index of Persons, these entries refer to land held before 1066 in the reign of King Edward.[1] They indicate clearly that land and wealth redistribution was not an innovation introduced after the Norman Conquest, but that it was customary to reward certain notable high-ranking commanders following foreign conquests with extensive wealth through land-holdings, which would also have the effect of absorbing them and their followers into the English realm. This absorption of foreign invaders from Northern Europe, Scandinavia and Gaul was a continuing phenomenon throughout the latter part of the tenth century. Once absorbed into the English nations, they were converted and evangelised to Christianity. It is therefore a fact that the so-called 'Anglo-Saxon' nation is better described as a Saxon-Danish-Scandinavian society, set apart by its English Christian royal identity, which has not been given its true historic value by a series of histories that have no well-documented basis for a balanced understanding of this period of English history.

This migration of peoples from the continental mainland to the north-west corner of Europe has never been satisfactorily understood and is beyond the remit of this investigation. It is not necessary to fully evaluate the reasons for these migrations in the furtherance of this study, but to note that they were a considerable and important influence upon shaping the character and constitution of the British Isles and the English nation in the turbulent period of the second half of the tenth century. In this regard, we can understand the Norman invasion as part of a cumulative movement of conquest and colonisation that continued long after the Conqueror's demise until the reign of Henry III in 1207.

For the brief period of Canute's reign, he was sometimes regarded as the King of a northern European empire: Emperor as well as King of England. He became a newly baptised Christian of predominately Danish descent. Danish custom and Danish law was established in the counties of East Anglia at least three hundred years before the reign of Canute. Many senior magnates and noblemen were of mixed race. Earl Godwin, Harold's father, was a confidante and admirer of Canute and although of ancient Anglo-Saxon lineage and ancestry, all his children were given Danish or Scandinavian names. Tostig, Harold's brother, fought with Hardrada at Stanford Bridge, probably with the promise of the English throne in the event of a Scandinavian victory. This is illustrative of the northern European dimension, of which, as a Norman, William was a major force, but nonetheless part of a much wider movement of conquest, with the British Isles as a very desirable and vulnerable group of islands ripe for plunder, conquest and colonisation.

If we examine the land-holdings of the Godwin family and Thorkell the Tall before 1066, there is a clear pattern that emerges in support of the record of the Godwin family's retreat to the West Country where their ancestral Wessex holdings provided a means of retreat, and, via the island of Steep Holm in the Severn estuary, a place of comparative safety in the island priory. It is also recorded in the Chronicle that Harold's sons from their base in Dublin harried the coastline, inciting the city of Bristol to support an English uprising against their Norman opponents. This attempt failed, but reveals the holdings of the Godwin family as a network of possible manorial support and shows clearly that Queen Edith, Harold's elder sister and King Edward's widow, was also dispossessed of some land, namely Puritan-owned by Saint Peter's Church, Rome, which was sequestered by King William. It is probable that Queen Edith administered this holding, which did not pay taxes, and therefore, we can infer, paid revenue directly to the Roman Church of Saint Peter. The Anglo-Saxon Wessex Domesday record includes significant holdings belonging before 1066 to Harold's daughters, who succeeded his father when he died on 15 April 1053.

The following information is taken from Domesday Book Index of Persons.[2] The records are only included where the Domesday Book clearly identifies the person as the daughter of King Harold, or in the case of Edith as 'puella'.

Harold's daughter Gytha has the following holdings recorded: 25 parcels of land, four manorial holdings in Cornwall and one in Dorset. These holdings are probably bequests from her grandfather after whose wife, Gytha Sprakeleg, she was named. Her grandmother was known as Countess Gytha and also had holdings in Devon and Cornwall; she is also recorded as Thorkelsdottir (daughter of Thorkell) and is referred to as a Danish princess. Thorkell the Tall was of a later generation and is distinguished by the descriptive appendix 'the Tall'. Gytha's remaining twenty holdings were spread across Oxford, Northampton, Warwickshire, Leicester, Lincoln and Yorkshire. These lands were adjacent to properties of Queen Edith, Edith the Fair and Rich, wife of Harold, and, critically, in Yorkshire, to Alan the Count of Brittany. By comparison, her younger sister Gunhild had sixteen holdings in the following counties: Sussex, Somerset, Berkshire, Cornwall, Devon, Hereford and Wiltshire. These lands were in the heartlands of the Earl Godwin, her grandfather and her father, Harold. Harold was born in Sussex, and she is referred to as his daughter in the Somerset record.

However, their mother, Edith the fair and rich, in addition to the extensive lands indicated above centred on Cambridgeshire, held over forty other manorial holdings in eleven other southern counties, extending from Middlesex to Cornwall. Her lands were the most extensive recorded for any woman in the realm and are far greater than her mother-in-law's holdings.

Countess Gytha, wife of Count Godwin and mother of King Harold, held before 1066: forty holdings in Cornwall, Devon, Somerset, Dorset, Hampshire, the Isle of Wight, Wiltshire, Sussex, Berkshire, Bedfordshire, Buckinghamshire, Derbyshire and Nottinghamshire.

If the supposition is correct that Edith the Fair is Thorkell's daughter by Wulfgyth, former wife of Ulfcytel and daughter of King Aethelred, then Edith would have been his heir and inherited all his English estates, making her a fabulously wealthy and powerful heiress. However as Harold's wife, following his defeat at the Battle of Hastings, she eventually fled to Denmark and the protection of the family of her father,

Thorkell the Tall, a Jomsviking warrior. Thorkell the Tall, although often thought of as a Danish Viking invader, had even greater land-holdings, as follows.

Thorkell the Tall owned land in 24 counties south of a line from the Humber to Gloucestershire, comprising over 145 estates; these lands must have been granted to him by King Canute and are indicative of the integration of Danish magnates into the English ruling class before 1040. However, it is noteworthy that Thorkell the Tall had no recorded land in Cambridgeshire, which supports the contention that Edith inherited these lands from her posthumous father, Ulfcytel, killed by Thorkell the Tall at the Battle of Assundan; this inheritance could be used to support the fact that she was Ulfcytel's daughter rather than the daughter of Thorkell the Tall. This is a matter that cannot be resolved with any certainty, but either way demonstrates a more equal status for women than that which prevailed following the Norman Conquest, especially in the matter of inherited wealth.

Primogeniture is Norman codification and a mistaken extension of the Canon Law regarding Christian marriage, which in the case of Queen Matilda's claim to the English throne as the grandchild of King William was in opposition to the sole or prime right of male inheritance. The daughters of Harold and Edith, as demonstrated above, in the manner of Anglo Saxon/Danish custom of noble inheritance, have fairly large land-holdings, some of which after careful analysis would appear to have been bequeathed through the female as well as the male line, especially grandmother, mother and daughter. This is best understood by Gunhilda's claim on the lands of her mother, Edith, in relation to her abduction by and marriage to Count Alan of Brittany.

A note of caution and explanation is necessary regarding any conclusions I have drawn from an analysis of the work of the Domesday Book Index of Persons. The personal names taken from the Latin text are recorded initially in a form of code. They have become distorted by phonetic modifications made by Norman-educated clerks when transposing German, Danish, Norse, Welsh, Breton, Irish and Biblical names taken from the Koine/Latin texts of Northern European origin. There is at present no etymological work available. However, I have limited my search to textual evidence, which clearly indicates by reference to the person in question in relation to family or other titles such as count of, wife of, son of and such like where there is compelling evidence of personal identification. As we examine the family and dynastic relationships from the reign of King Canute through to the Conqueror's reign from 1066 to 1088 in regard to the Lady of Walsingham, there emerges a pattern of high ranking and royal court relationships that have far-reaching European connections.

The north European Germanic/Anglo-Saxon settlers were under constant pressure from at least the fifth century. From Alfred's reign throughout the tenth century, the Scandinavian peoples, together with the Gauls, were repelled and absorbed into the very rich economy of the British Isles. The many thousands of miles of coastline and inland riverine systems were impossible to defend against all-comers. By the tenth century, after at least seven hundred years of this conglomerate of nations, it was identified within its ruling hierarchies and ideas of government by the Christian Gospel revelation.

Century followed century and the last Scandinavian conqueror, Canute, was baptised with the Holy Cross on its discovery at Montecanute as a personal revelation or trigger to his conversion. He bequeathed the church and the Holy Cross to the protection of Harold and, following King Harold Harefoot and King Edmond, to the patronage of Saint Edward the Confessor and the Anglo-Saxon Christian heritage built upon the martyrs, Alban and Aaron and Julius, was brought into the Western Patriarchy and gradually lost its Orthodox identity, which can be traced back to the Church of Hippo, of Antioch and Alexandria. This Christian identity of the English Church was established in the kingdom of Wessex, the seat of Alfred the Great's power base; Saint Bede was unable to find a circle of correspondents from the West, and this failure has ensured an unbalanced and erroneous understanding of the Anglo-Saxon Church in its fullness. This study of the identity of the Visionary of Walsingham has allowed me to shine a little light on the English Church prior to the conquest of 1066.

Notes

1 J. M. Dodgson and J. J. Palmer (eds), *Domesday Book Index of Persons* (Chichester: Phillimore, 1992). Alphabetical index and by county.

2 *Ibid.*

Appendix B

The Will of Wulfgyth

Archive, Canterbury Cathedral Christ Church (AD 1044–1053; possibly 1046).[1]

Text

Hyer suotelet bisen ywrite hu Wolgyb yan hire bing efter hire worbisbe be hire sealmighti God yube on liue to brukene: bet is panne erest mine lhouerde hid rigte heriet and ic yan bet land at at Stistede a Godes ywitnesse and mine vrenden into Christes chereche, ba muneken to uostre. On ban yrede bet Elfkitel and Kytelmine bea \ r/n bruke bas londes hyre dey. And sebben gange bet land into christes chereche buten eccherenagentale, vor mien saule and vor Elfwines mines blouand vor alre mine bierne and by hialue be men vrye efter here dage. And icy an into bare chereche at Stistede. To ban bic ic on liue yube. Eldemes land and bertohveken bet ber sv alles vifty ekeres on wode on velde efter mine forbsibe. And icy an Wolkitele and Kytele minen suns bet land at Walsingeham and at Karltun and Herlingham. And icy an minen twam dogtren, Gode and Bote, Sexlingham and Sumerledetune and into bare chereche at Somerletune sixteen eker londes and /enne\ eker med. And ic van Ealebye mine dogter het land at Gheartekere and at Essetesford and bane wde be ic leyde berto. And ic van Godwyne eorle and Harold eorle Fribetune. And icy an into Cristes Chereche to Cristes weuede ane littleune geldene rode and ane setregal. And icy an seynte Edmunde tueyen ybonede hornes. And icy an Seynte Ebeldithe ane pellerne kertel. And icy an seynte Osythe half pund fees. And be geue mine barnes. And icy an Seynte Austine ane regragel And se be mine quyde beryaui be hic nu biqueben habbe a Godes ywitnesse beryaued he worbe bises erthliche mergbes and ashiregihine se almigti Drigten, be alle shepbe shop and and ywrogte, vram alrehalegene ymmenesse on domesday, and sy be bytagt Satane bane diefle and alle his awarvede yueren into helle grunde, and ber aquelmi <mid> godes wibsaken bute ysuyke and mine irfnumen neuer ne asuenche bisses is to ywitnesse Edward King and manie obre.

This edition: Charters of Christ Church Canterbury (Brooks and Kelly, Anglo Saxon Charters, no 176).

Transliteration

In this document it is made known that after her death Wulfgyth will bequeath her things which Almighty God has given her to take joy in for her use in this life. This is firstly to my Lord his due Heriot. The estate at Stisted [in Essex] I grant with the witness of God and my friends, to Christ Church to the support of the monks on condition that Aelfketel [Ulfketel] and Ketel, my children, may have the full use of during their days here. Afterwards the estate then will pass to Christ Church without any hindrance or dispute. For the soul of me and my Lord Aelfwine and for the souls of all my children and after their day half the men in service to be made freemen. That is free of any kind of Hidage. And to the Church at Stisted as well as I that which I gave when alive, I give together with land adjoining that there will be in all fifty acres of woodland and open meadow pasture when I die. And I give to Ulfketel and Ketel mine own sons, the Estates at Walsingham and at Carleton and Herlingham [in Norfolk]. And I give to my two daughters, Goda and Bote, Saxlingham [Suffolk],

Somerleytun [Somerton, Suffolk], and to the church at Sumerleytun sixteen acres of [plough] land and one acre meadow. And I give to Eadygo my daughter the land at Cheartekere [Chadacre] [Suffolk] and at Essetesforde together with the wood I added thereto. And I give Earl Godwin and Earl Harold, Fritton [Suffolk]. And I grant to Christes Church for the Altar of Christ a small Golden Cross and Chalice cover. And I grant to Bury Saint Edmund's church two decorated candelabra. And I give to Saint Ethelthrith's [Ely] a purple priestly vestment. And I grant to Saint Oswyth's half a pound in coin to be paid annually by my children. And I grant to Saint Augustine's a dorsal stand [possibly for supporting an incense thurifer whilst not in use]. And let him who may despoil my will which I have now made known before you in the witness of Almighty God who created all things and made all creatures exclude him from the Saints on the Day of Judgement. And may he descend to the abyss of hell to Satan the devil and all his accursed companions and there suffer as opponents of God without end. And may God protect my heirs from such affliction.

To this King Edward is witness with many others. [BWF].

Will of Eadygo [E]go Godwin and Wulfgyth

Translation

Edith Godwine and Wulfgyth, Grant land at Stisted and Coggeshall in Essex to Christ's Church Canterbury In the time and before King Edward who reigns under God the Father and his son Jesus. These gifts are given freely and absolutely without constraint to the Church for the Greater Glory of God.

Text

[E]go Godwinus et Wlthgif, concedente et consentiente domino meo rege Eduuardo, donamus ecclesie Christi in

Dorobernia aliquam partem terre uiris nostri nomine Stigestede et Coggashaele Eastseaxa, liberas ab omni seculari seruitute, sicut ego a prefato domino meo rege Eaduuardo, et a patre ejuis hactenus tenui. Si qui eas a iure eiusdem ecclesie abstulerit, auferat ei Deus Gloriam suam.

This will of Wulfgyth clearly illuminates a great many important issues which have been contentious and mistaken by a number of commentators, and especially popular writers of history. The corrupted or damaged text '[E]go' Godwinus should probably be understood as the scribal abbreviation of Eadygo, that is, Edith or Edeva, and underlines the family bonds between the Godwins and the family of Wulfgyth. Some interpreters have assumed that this name refers to Queen Edith, wife of King Edward; however, she would bear the title or her spouse's family name and not that of Godwin, her maiden name. It implies that Edith was married to Harold in *c.* 1044, having been born around 1018–1022 and shows how King Edward was involved in their close relationship especially of Edith to Christ's Church at Canterbury.

The witness of the reigning monarch, Edward the Confessor, indicates Wulfgyth's royal lineage and closeness to the Crown of England at the end of the Anglo-Saxon period.

This evidence of royal connection suggests strongly that she was half-sister to Edward, being the daughter of Aethelred by his second wife. It is clear through the naming of her two sons, Ulfketel and Ketel, that in all probability she had been married to Ulfcytel, the great English general who died at Assundan in 1017, defeated by Cnut and his Danish Jomsviking Commander, Thorkell the Tall. There is a great deal of evidence from both English and Danish sources that she, as a widow, married Thorkell, who is recorded in Scandinavian sources as having killed Ulfcytel during the battle at Assundan. According to material later added to the Icelandic volume of the Flateyjarbok, Ulfcytel was married to a daughter of Aethelred, Wulfhilda, and after his death she married Thorkell.

In these often-brutal times, marriage to the victor sometimes took place in the case of a noble widow with a young family: the man became 'protector in honour' of the vanquished. There have been many writers who have, on no substantial evidence, believed that Thorkell the Tall married Edith, wife of Eric Streona, in the same or following year of the battle of Assundan. This is unlikely for a number of reasons. The first and most compelling of these is the fact that Eric Streona was executed for treachery by King Cnut after the battle of Assundan; his treachery cost many lives on both sides during this battle, in which he failed to commit his forces. Had he committed his forces to either side, they would have had a numerical advantage and would have probably been victorious. His failure to commit his forces had the consequence of prolonging the combat and increasing the slaughter on both sides. His decision not to join the fray was designed to present himself with the opportunity of claiming the spoils of victory without combat, which would have left him with a very powerful voice, as he then claimed for whoever who had the victory. This covert action of treachery was calculated to promote his interests without risk, and he was duly decapitated on the order of King Cnut the following year; he was the victor, together with Thorkell the Tall his commander and Jomsviking mentor; however, the treachery of Streona contributed greatly to the death of many English nobles.

In these circumstances, it is highly unlikely that Thorkell would contemplate marriage to a traitor's widow and difficult to understand why King Cnut would sanction such a union. It was following the battle of Assundan that Cnut became the English king, and it was for his treachery to the English faction that Eric Streona was beheaded. Further, it is highly unlikely that Thorkell, a Dane, would have met Eric Streona. Eric Streona's estates were situated in the north-west, an area Thorkell the Tall never visited. Contrast this with Wulfhilda, the widow of Ulfcytel, whose family background (together with his widow) was as part of the ruling nobility of the Danelaw.

In her will, Wulfgyth reveals that Great and Little Walsingham are part of her holdings and their proximity to Cnut's estates adjoining them, based on Wells on Sea, which passed to King Edward; again, this indicates her own royal connection with King Aethelred. It also explains beyond doubt how Walsingham became a family estate of the Godwin's through Edith's mother, Wulfgyth, and her daughter, Edith, and sons, Ulfketel and Ketel. Wulfgyth's testament, as shown above, includes a reference to her 'Lord Aelfwine'. This is probably a reference to her 'Lord Bishop Aelfwine' who was Bishop of North Elmenham, which is twelve miles from Walsingham. He was bishop from 1019 to 1023, and after the Conquest the diocese was translated (amidst much controversy) to Thetford and then to Norwich. Bishop Aelfwine died in 1023. He was a monk at Ely, and his parents and land gifts are listed in the Liber Eliensis. In 1024 and 1044, Bishop Stigand was for a short period bishop of North Elmenham before he was translated to Winchester and then soon after to Canterbury.

Notes

1 N. P. Brookes and S. E. Kelly (eds.), *Charters of Christ Church Canterbury* (Oxford: Oxford University Press, 2013), number 176.

Appendix C

Norfolk Western Hundreds

This map of the Western Hundreds shows the landholders of the LDB 1066–1088 numbered according their location in the Norfolk Hundreds, together with the attached tabulation indexed through the numbers to the name referred to in the LDB and the specific title-holder in 1066.[1]

These holdings of King Edward and Harold were in King Williams's jurisdiction; they are numbered and circled in the North Greenhow Hundred and the adjoining Gallow Hundred. The jurisdiction prior to the Conquest is shown as either King Edward's or Harold's.

The map numbering and the Hundred borders are all taken from the LDB. The North Greenhow Hundred was divided in the reign of Canute, when, under the settlements of the Danelaw in these parts of East Anglia, the population increased considerably with the expansion of the acreage of arable land cultivated. The North Greenhow Hundred has the sea port of Wells-next-the-Sea shown as a holding of King Edward, which was formerly held by Canute. The honour manorial holding was Wighton, still assessed partly in terms of its 'food tribute', and of course the major manorial holding in the Hundred, belonging to King Edward. As is clearly indicated on this map, the adjoining Hundred of Gallow has been taken from the

North Greenhow Hundred and extends along its western boundaries from (20) Stibbard and (21) 'Little' Ryburgh to the coast (1) and (2) Burnham Overy and Burnham Thorpe. Twelve of the 21 holdings in Gallow are in Harold's name; most importantly Harold also held Great Walsingham and Little and Great Snoring in the North Greenhow Hundred.

However, it is recorded in the will of Wulfhilda, who was probably Edith's mother, that she and her sons, Ketel and Ulfketel, whose father Ulfcytel was respected as the English leader who defended Cambridge, that they held Great and Little Walsingham and Great Snoring.

This part of the Danelaw from 950 to 1066 was of great strategic importance, hence the holdings held in the names of both Canute and Edward. This is indicated in the reigns of King Aethelred and King Canute, and from these holdings we can see clearly how close the family of Harold was to both kings. It also indicates clearly how the family of Edith was firmly entrenched in Great and Little Walsingham; her mother also had close ties with Aelfwine, the Bishop of Elmenham, and more importantly her will concerning in part the Walsingham holdings is signed by King Edward.

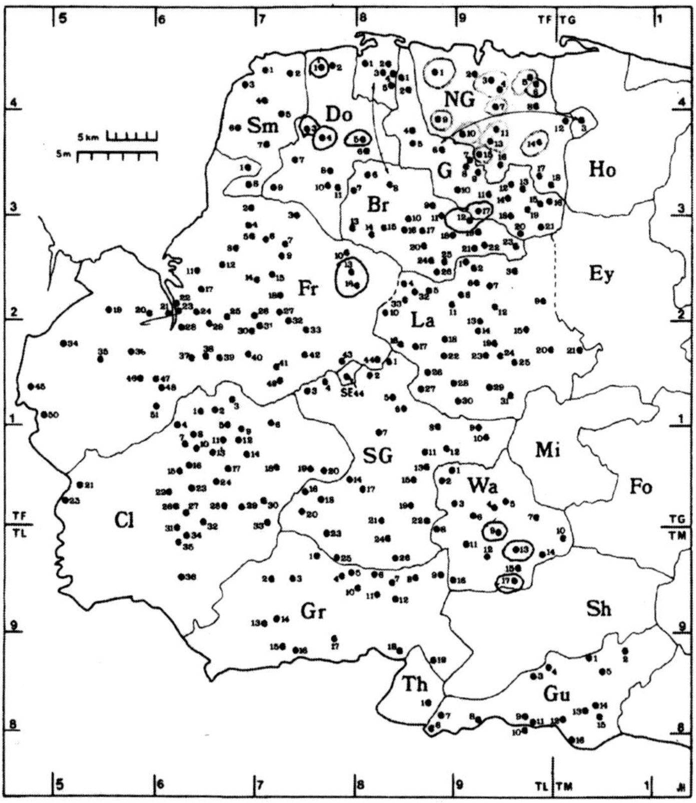

NORFOLK WESTERN HUNDREDS

Norfolk Western Hundreds

Settlements identified with data taken from the Ordnance Survey Map.

Gallow Hundred (Greenhow)

(1) Burnham Overy—Harold
(2) Burnham Thorpe—Harold
(3) Saxdringham—Harold
(4) Creake North—Outlier
(5) Creake South—Outlier
(6) Waterden—Not identified
(7) North Barsham—Not identified
(8) East Barsham—Not identified
(9) West Barsham—Not identified
(10) East Barsham—Not identified
(11) Little Snoring—Outlier
(12) Kettlestone—Outlier
(13) Alethorpe—Outlier of Fakenham
(14) Croxton—Not identified
(15) Croxton—Not identified
(16) Croxton—Not identified
(17) Fulmodeston—Not identified
(18) Fakenham—Harold
(19) Pensthorpe—Not identified
(20) Clipstone—Not identified
(21) Little Ryburgh—Not identified
(22) Stibbard—Not identified.

North Greenhow Hundred

(23) Holkham—King Edward
(24) Wells-next-to-Sea—King Edward
(25) Warham St. Mary—Not identified
(26) Warham All Saints—Not identified

(27) Stiffkey—King Edward
(28) Cock Thorpe—Not identified
(29) Wighton honour court manor—King Edward
(30) Binham—Not identified
(31) Quarles—King Edward
(32) Egmere—King Edward
(33) Great Walsingham—Harold
(34) Field Dalling—King Edward
(35) Little Walsingham—Harold
(36) Hindringham—King Edward
(37) Houghton St. Giles—King Edward [Murlais]
(38) Great Snoring—Harold
(39) Thursford—Not identified
(40) Barney—Not identified

The ordnance survey map and the tables show the close interweaving of settlements in this very small area, as land-holding under the jurisdiction of King Edward the Confessor and King Harold. This pattern so clearly shown also underlines the verisimilitude of the evidence of the family manors of Ketel and Ulfketel as well as their mother Wulfhilda and half-sister, Edith, in Walsingham. Although they were recorded under Harold's name in the LDB the evidence of Wulfhida's will, signed and attested by King Edward, show that these were her lands and refer to Bishop Aelfwine of Elmenham as her Spiritual Lord; this reflects the probability of her royal status as the daughter of King Aethelred.

Notes

1 S. Morris (ed.), *Domesday Book, Norfolk* (Chichester: Phillimore, 1984).

Appendix D

Plan, plates, figures of St Laurence Chapel & Friary

Figure 1: St Laurence's Chapel[1]

Figure 2: Chapel roof

Figure 3: relevant seals

Key: (top left) the earliest seal showing the Priory with tower; (top right) the badge of Our Lady of Rocamadour; (bottom left) later seal of Walsingham (obverse side); (bottom left) later seal, showing Our Lady seated with the emblem of the tree of Jesse with Christ pointing to the Isaiah citation. Our Lady is wearing the Davidic Crown enthroned with the scroll back throne depicting the seven commandments.[2]

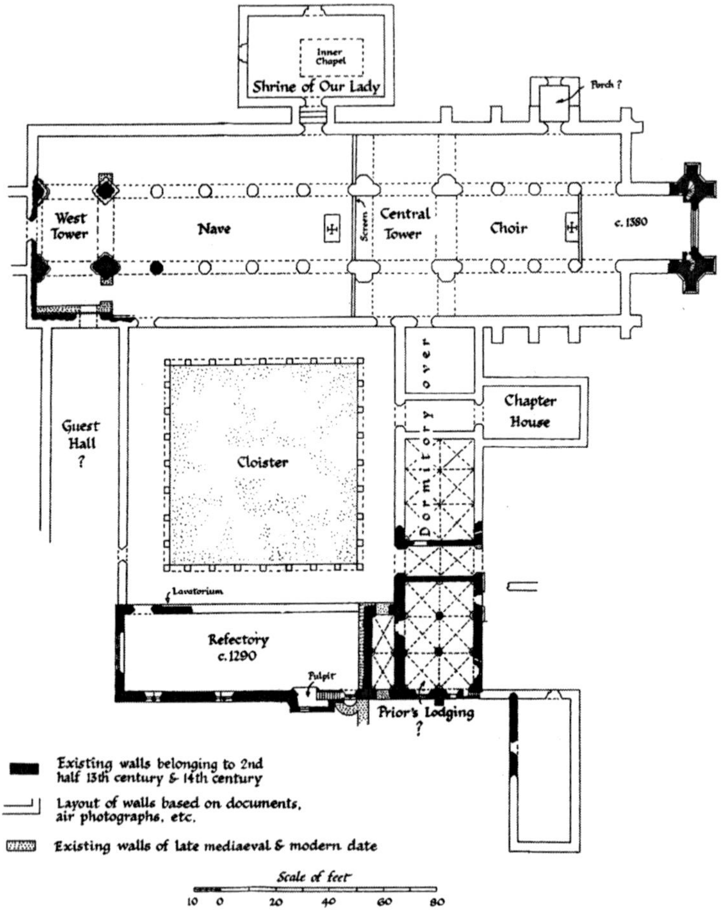

Figure 4: Ground plan of the Priory[3]

Notes

1 J. C. Dickinson, *The Shrine of Our Lady of Walsingham* (Cambridge: Cambridge University Press, 1956), plate 3, figure (b).

2 *Ibid.*, plates 5 and 6.

3 *Ibid.*, plate facing page 106.

Postscript

Poem

May we go to Walsingham

To Joseph and Mary's House

by

Bill Flint

The House of the Holy Family
Came in a dream to Edith,
Fair and richly favoured, servant of the Lord,
A vision proclaimed by angels and the Holy Ghost.

They built the house, then moved it on,
For angels foretold them the ground was wrong,
Hard by the wells where healing water flowed,
The house of Joseph and Mary came to England.

This England, Mary's dowry, her land of hope,
Her island decked out in blossom silk
Where the woods and sea meet on the Norfolk coast,
Jesus' house was built through prayer by the Saxon Cross,
The cross of the lowland sheep,
The wide lands of the Norfolk folds.

Edward the Confessor prayed to her,
The Mother of God, our Dowry Queen,
The Danes and Norman fighting men brought war,
They plundered England, Our Lady's garden,
And left a legacy of legal pomp and splendour.

Walsingham remains Our Lady's posy,
Her house, this place of prayer, this is where she reigns,
Where the May and the Blackthorn bloom,
Where the dove calls and Bede wrote
Of the table laid and the sparrow watched in flight.

BIBLIOGRAPHY

THIS BIBLIOGRAPHY IS provided to establish the sources of the main body of the evidence and to allow the reader to more fully appreciate the overlying exposition and reasoning in support of my main conclusions. The emphasis, as the title of the work indicates, is to reveal the person described in the Shrine's histories as the Lady of the Manor of Walsingham in 1061, referred to in many documents as Richeldis Faverches. However, the surname or family name is of modern origin and has as its reference the Norfolk Rolls that refers not to the Shrine's Visionary founder, but to a familial place-name in Normandy, possibly near Lisieux.

The main body of evidence is recorded in the Domesday books for Norfolk, Cambridgeshire, Suffolk, Essex and the Burgess holdings in Fakenham, Norwich, Colchester and Canterbury.

The major general historical studies I have used are the works of F. M. Stenton, Barlow and the Chronicles, where applicable and available.

F. M. Stenton, *Anglo Saxon England* (Oxford: Oxford University Press, 1962).

This general study remains a significant work for understanding this complex period in the development of the English state. The passages relevant to this study are Chapters X, XIV and XVIII; this introduces the reader to the events at the time of the early history of the Shrine, from the reign of King Canute until the departure of the Conqueror in 1086 and the publication of the Norfolk edition of the Little Domesday book. Chapter XII provides an introduction to the events that shaped Anglo-Saxon and Danish society, providing an overview, although restricted in geographical terms, to the southern regions of Mercia, Wessex and East Anglia. Chapter XVIII covers the reorganisation of the English Church under Archbishop Lanfranc and provides an insight into the Norfolk ecclesiastical pre-Norman Episcopacy of the Cathedral of Elmenham. Without royal approval provided by the foundation date of King Edward's reign, the Walsingham Shrine would not have been provided with guardianship of Geoffrey the pious relation of the Count of Brittany's extended family.

The most important source material for this project has been the Domesday Survey, especially the Little Domesday book of Norfolk, Suffolk and Essex completed in 1088.

The Domesday Book, ed. P. Brown (general editor J. Morris) (Chichester: Phillimore, 1984) Norfolk, Suffolk, Essex and Cambridgeshire.

These are important source documents for this study and the records, tables, indices and maps are invaluable. They provide at the beginning of each volume the definitive list of landholders who were given land under the king. Norman society under William was a strict, inflexible hierarchy. This provides the student with a complete list of landholders under the crown. All were subject to the crown and the itemised holdings indicate the Hundred in which the territory is situated. The complete listing of Norman Magnates includes bishops, abbots and the name of the holder of these lands before 1066.

The final pages of each county volume provide an index of place-names and persons. This can be cross-referenced against listings of church holdings and clergy and be used, by reference to the index of places, to provide, with the maps available, a geographical and topographical understanding of major landholders such as Count Alan of Brittany and other high-ranking and powerful supporters of the king. In the completion of this study of the Visionary of the Shrine of Walsingham, the Domesday records have proved invaluable. If in future this work is carried out on a county and regional basis, it will provide most detailed and useful historical information which flows back down the historical stream through to the ancient administrative and social settings which illuminate the vibrancy and tenacity of English society especially within the social and compassionate embrace of the Christian church.

The Anglo-Saxon Chronicles, ed. Dorothy Whitelock (London: Eyre and Spottiswode, 1961).

This source book is invaluable in translation but requires specialist knowledge and must be interpreted with a range of wide reading and careful appraisal of the bias and limited scope of many passages. Their chronology and authorship reflects the clerical writer's limitations and with regard to the events narrated, they are clearly written as propaganda in order to sustain the ruling dynasty in a favourable light. Also written by ecclesiastical appointees, they were written to convey the unique understanding of these events as religious history within the prevailing understanding of Christ's providential guidance. In many instances this is an invaluable and unique source of information, and where it is possible to cross-reference major events it is often reliable, but with a pessimistic evaluation of outcomes and damage to the sovereign body.

Frank Barlow, *The English Church 1000–1066* (London: Methuen, 1970).

Although this is an informed and forthright history, it requires careful analysis in its major assumptions and conclusions. The chapters dealing with monastic reform and the influence of the English Benedictine Order, especially on trade, town and the parochial liturgy, are contentious and should be examined together with the work of Abbott Gasquet, *Parish Life in Medieval England* (London: Kessinger, 1907).

Encomium Emmae Reginae, ed. Alistair Campbell (Cambridge: Cambridge University Press, 1949).

Although this is a biased source book, it is useful in understanding the specific episodes under review. It should be used with caution when evaluating the specifics of familial relationships as they impact on the English Crown and court.

Simon Keynes, 'Canute's Earls', in Alexander Rumble (ed.), The Reign of Cnut: King of England, Denmark and Norway (Leicester: Leicester University Press, 1994).

There is in this volume an insightful and informed account of the intricate relationship between the King and his powerful regional earls; this is especially useful in gaining an understanding of his relations with Thorkell the Tall, Eric Streona and King Cnut.

Alexander Nazarenko, *Gytha wife of Vladimir II Monomakh* (Moscow: Русский фонд содействия образованию и науке, 2001).[1]

This work is essential to an understanding of the life of Gytha, daughter of King Harold II of England and Edith the Fair.

A. Nazarenko, *Древняя Русь на международных путях ('Old Rus on international roads', published in English as International Relations of Ancient Rus)* (Moscow: Русский фонд содействия образованию и науке, 2001).

Catholic Encyclopaedia (CDRom)

This is a source book for many enquiries regarding Rome and European ecclesiastic affairs as they impacted England under Norman rule.

K. S. B. Keats Rohan, *Domesday People* (London: Boydell Press, 1999), pp. 380, 396–398.

I. J. Sanders, *English Baronies* (Oxford: Oxford University Press, 1963), pp. 12, 46–7.

Letters and Papers, Foreign and Domestic, Henry VIII, Vol. 1 (1509–1514), No 4373, ed. J. S. Brewer (London: HM Stationery Office, 1920).

Pamela A. Neville, *Richard Pynson Printer (1506–1529)* (London: University of London, 1990).

Pamela A. Neville, *Printing and Propaganda in Early Tudor England,* dissertation, London (1990).

Pamela A. Neville, *Richard Pynson, Glover and Printer* 'The Library', 4th series, (3) 1922/23, pp. 49–51.

Emma Mason, *St. Wulfstan of Worcester c. 1008–1095* (Cambridge, Mass.: Basil Blackwood, 1990).

Florence: Florentis Wigorniensis, Monachi. Chronichi ex Chronicis, ed. Benjamin Thorpe, S.A.S., Vol. 1, London (1848).

Snorre Thulurson, *Norges kongesagaer* (Oslo: Gylendal Norsk Forlag, 1979).

Thietmar of Memeburg Ottonian Germany, translated by David A. Warner (Manchester: Manchester University Press, 2001).

Frank Barlow, *The Feudal Kingdom of England 1042–1016* (Harlow: Longman, 1955), pp. 71–98.

Susan. J. Ridyard, *The Royal Saints of Anglo Saxon England: A Study of West Saxon and East Anglian Cults.* Part of Cambridge Studies in Medieval thought (Cambridge: Cambridge University Press, 2008).

D. Knowles D. and R. N. Hadcock, *Medieval Religious Houses, England and Wales,* 2nd edn. (Harlow: Longman, 1971).

W. Farrer, Feudal Cambridgeshire (Cambridge: Cambridge University Press, 1920).

W. Levison, *England and the Continent in the Eighth century. The Ford lectures delivered in the Hilary term 1943* (Oxford: Clarendon, 1943).

H. E. J. Cowdery, 'Pope Gregory VII and the Anglo Norman Church and kingdom', Studio Gregoriani (1972), pp. 60–204.

For an early study of the history of Wilton Convent see *The Life of King Edward the Confessor,* translated and edited by F. Barlow (Bungay, Suffolk: Methuen, 1962) pp. 96–100.

Gunhild may have returned to the Wilton Convent, as recorded by William of Malmesbury in *Vita Wulfstani* edited by R. R. Darlington (Worcester: Camden Society, 1928). Wulfstan was spiritual adviser to King Harold II and very close to the Godwin family; therefore his testimony should be understood as a probably sympathetic response, although in my judgement an accurate and true testimony to the facts as then known.

M. T. Clanchy, *England and its Rulers 1066–1072* (Oxford: Blackwell, 1982).

Papal Bull; Eugenius III issued from Vetralla Dec 1st 1145; addressed to Louis King of France.

History of the Crusades, vol. I, ed. M. Bolin and K. Sutton (University of Wisconsin Press, 1919), pp. 474–478.

Scandinavian England ed. F. T. Wainwright and H. P. R. Finberg (Chichester: Phillimore, 1975).

Catholic Encyclopaedia, article on 'Canons and Canonesses Regular'.

Bullarium Laterense (Rome: 1727). Penmoto, Generalis Soari Ordinus Clericanium Canonicarium Hispania Tripartium (Rome 1642) Amort, Vertus Discipinia, Canonici Regularis, Benvenuti Discoso sterico—teologico della vita commune Dei Cricerici dei primi dedici saecoli della chessa (1728).

Molinet Sur 1, origine 1 et antiquite clericais secularis de regularis.

D. Scully, *The Life of the Venerable Thomas a Kempis* (London: Methuen, 1904).

Addamman of Iona, *Life of Columba, founder of Hy,* ed. V. Reeves (Edinburgh: Penguin Press, 1958).

Chronicle of English Canonesses, ed. A. Hamilton (London: Louvain, 1898).

H. A. Cronne, *The Reign of Stephen* (London: Weidenfeld and Nicolson, 1970).

Leland, J. *Joannis Lelandi Antiquarii De Rebus Collectanea*, T. Hearne (ed.) (London, 1715). Bodleian Library, Oxford 111, 26.

S. Coleman and J. Elsner, *Pilgrimage Past and Present: Sacred Travel and Sacred Space in the World Religions* (London: British Museum Press and Cambridge MA: Harvard University Press, 1995).

C. R. Dodwell, *The Pictorial Art of the West* (New Haven: Yale University Press, 1993) pp. 193–4, 211–215, 800–1200.

The first representations of the passage from Isaiah from *c.* 1000 AD in the West show a shoot in the form of a straight stem on a flowering branch held in the hand of (most often) of the Virgin; Jesus sometimes, when held by Mary, points to the Virgin with this flowering stem. Sometimes the stem is held by an ancestor as revealed in Matthew and Luke's genealogies. The shoot as an attribute reminded the beholder that Mary of the House of Jesse is a primary part of the fulfilment of the prophecy. In the Byzantine world, the tree only appears as a reminder of the prophecy. 'The New Testament hidden in the Old Testament and revealed in Word of God of the Gospels.' The Tree in the background is also part of the iconography of the Nativity scenes. The Tree and the Green man are far more numerous in northern Europe and may have originated among the Anglo-Saxon peoples. These early icons are shown on p. 14; on p. 16, Jesus points to the flowering stem of the Jesse Tree held by Mary, who is crowned with the Davidic Coronet, as in the Walsingham seals and statue.

G. Schiller, *Iconography of Christian Art*, vol. I, translated from the German by J. Seligman (London: Lund Humphries, 1971) Plate K-22 & Figs 17–42.

E. Male, *The Gothic Image, Religious Art in France of the Thirteenth Century* (London: Collins, 1973), pp. 165–8. See *Sermon 24*, of Saint Leo the Great:

> In which rod no doubt, the Blessed Virgin Mary is predicted. Who sprung from the stock of Jesse and David and was fecundated by the Holy Spirit. Brought forth a new flower of human flesh becoming a Virgin Mother.

Thus a saintly pope and doctor of the church reveals to us the glories of revelation and the gifts of the Holy Spirit resplendent in the iconography of the Walsingham Statue of Our Lady and the Child Jesus.

A History of the County of Norfolk, vol. 2, ed. William Page (London: Boydell & Brewer, 1906), including W. Page, 'Hugh Bigot, 1135', p. 394.

Feudatory and Royal Steward testified that in his presence Henry I on his death bed disinherited his daughter and designated Stephen as his successor; Stephen was crowned on 22 December 1135.

See also p. 392: a reference to the foundation of the Shrine, referred to as a unique copy of the Pynson Ballad held in the Pepys Library dated to 1460, which states 'that the Chapel was founded in the Reign of Edward the Confessor'.

See also facing p. 394, plate facsimiles of Walsingham Priory Seals

1. Obverse: 'The Priory with central tower over the Nave and four turreted corner spires with windows as on plan indicating column towers.'
2. Reverse: 'Our Lady enthroned and crowned with seven Sacramental scrolls entwined on the back support uprights. She is holding in her hand the flowering branch from the Rod of Jesse.'
3. 'Seated on her left knee is the child Jesus presenting the open gospels with his left hand, as the Word made flesh. With his right hand he is reaching up and pointing to the Jesse Tree held by His mother, thus fulfilling the prophecy of the Old Testament as revealed in the New. Epistle to the Romans, Chapter 12, Verses 6–8.'

Notes

1 Published by the Russian foundation for co-operation in science and research. This is also the publisher for Nazarenko's other works mentioned here.

Index

Numbers in italics refer the reader to images, and 'n' after a page number refers to reader to an endnote.

Lightning Source UK Ltd.
Milton Keynes UK
UKOW04f0709231015

261194UK00003B/31/P

9 780852 448700